Industry Leaders' Reactions to
STOP WASTING WORDS

"Stop Wasting Words accomplishes what most books only aspire to. It provides truly unique insight on invisible drivers of each of our communication practices and success. And then it goes a step further to tell us all how to become more strategic and purposeful in our interactions. As the collaborative intensity of work has exploded this is more than a nicety for people today—it is a critical capability for professional and personal success."

ROB CROSS, *Edward A. Madden Professor of Global Leadership, Babson College; founder of Connected Commons*

"Effective, concise communication—now more than ever—is lost in the cacophony of meaningless and misused words coming from every possible direction. Cutting through the din with clear messages is essential for those striving for leadership positions. *Stop Wasting Words* provides a roadmap for those focused individuals who recognize that the message is nothing until the recipient understands what it says.

With decades of experience in the communication field, Eric Eisenberg and Sean Mahar know every facet of creative, impactful writing. This is a must-read book for everyone frustrated with ineffective missives and who wants to redirect the course of human interaction, one word at a time.

MOEZ LIMAYEM, *PhD, dean of the University of South Florida's Muma College of Business*

T0145687

"Over the past two decades Sean Mahar has been a tremendous resource for me in developing educational programs for health professionals and trainees both by sharing his deep insight into core principles of communication and by packaging them in very tangible and relevant exercises and examples. The full catalogue has been compiled here in collaboration with Eric Eisenberg. This should be the 'go-to' guide for people who want to succeed as organizational leaders."

MICHAEL PICCHIONI, *MD*

"Good and effective communication is the lifeblood of any organization and good communication skills are the hallmark of an effective leader. Over the years, I have tried to hone my skills as an effective communicator and wish that I had had access to a book like this early in my career. Beginning with a chapter on self assessment and humility, Dr. Eric Eisenberg and Mr. Sean Mahar take the reader through a way of listening, communicating, and seeking feedback that not only provides the basis for conscious communication but allows the reader to grow as an effective reader.

For me, being able to translate these skills through my entire organization and improve our communication skills is why this book will be required reading for our current and future leaders."

CHARLES L. D'AMOUR, *president and CEO, Big Y Supermarkets, Springfield, MA*

STOP WASTING WORDS

STOP WASTING WORDS

LEADING THROUGH CONSCIOUS COMMUNICATION

ERIC M. EISENBERG & SEAN E. MAHAR

Advantage®

Published by Advantage, Charleston, South Carolina.
Member of Advantage Media Group.

ADVANTAGE is a registered trademark, and the Advantage colophon is a trademark of Advantage Media Group, Inc.

Printed in the United States of America.

10 9 8 7 6 5 4 3 2 1

ISBN: 978-1-64225-128-9
LCCN: 2019912028

Book design by Carly Blake.

This publication is designed to provide accurate and authoritative information in regard to the subject matter covered. It is sold with the understanding that the publisher is not engaged in rendering legal, accounting, or other professional services. If legal advice or other expert assistance is required, the services of a competent professional person should be sought.

 Advantage Media Group is proud to be a part of the Tree Neutral® program. Tree Neutral offsets the number of trees consumed in the production and printing of this book by taking proactive steps such as planting trees in direct proportion to the number of trees used to print books. To learn more about Tree Neutral, please visit **www.treeneutral.com**.

Advantage Media Group is a publisher of business, self-improvement, and professional development books and online learning. We help entrepreneurs, business leaders, and professionals share their Stories, Passion, and Knowledge to help others Learn & Grow. Do you have a manuscript or book idea that you would like us to consider for publishing? Please visit **advantagefamily.com** or call **1.866.775.1696**.

PART ONE

Becoming Conscious of How You Communicate Today

"Zwischen Reiz und Reaktion liegt ein Raum. In diesem Raum liegt unsere Macht zur Wahl unserer Reaktion. In unserer Reaktion liegen unsere Entwicklung und unsere Freiheit."

"Between stimulus and response there is a space. In that space is our power to choose our response. In our response lies our growth and our freedom."

—VIKTOR E. FRANKL

CONTENTS

Acknowledgments

We wish to thank two groups of people:

- The communication scholars who have shared their insights to improve the quality of life for all people via more conscious communication.

- Those around the world who have performed military or government service out of a dedication to freedom for all men and women to read, write, and acquire the knowledge needed to improve their own lives and the lives of their neighbors.

Because of the courageous work of these two groups, we are free to share what we have learned and to help you to discover how conscious communication can improve your own life, the lives of your loved ones, and the lives of your organizations. With unconscious communication, every interaction with our friends, students, employees, and organizations is diminished. With conscious communication, there is no limit to the good that we can achieve.

Leadership as an Aspiration and a Journey

We write this book with a sense of urgency. Our world is confronting a range of megacrises, some of which threaten our habitat and survival as a species. Political discourse is more fragmented and contentious than at any time in recent memory. Organizational challenges make the headlines almost daily. Institutions and individuals struggle to survive amid relentless criticism on social media. It is in our best interest that we work together to discover and promote ways of communicating that foster peace and prosperity. Shifting from how we currently behave to new ways of relating to one another will require strong and courageous leadership.

Unfortunately, leadership is in short supply across every sector of every economy in the world today. We need better leaders in private industry, government, nonprofits, and education. We need better leaders everywhere. The good news is that some people *are* willing to step up. The bad news is that all too often they cannot do what is required of an effective leader.

Why is this? As a rule, individuals are selected for or elected to leadership positions based on technical excellence, not on demonstrated leadership skill. Predictably they discover that what stymies their long-term success as leaders is the inability to create and sustain effective interpersonal relationships. To state what should be obvious: Being able to perform a task oneself does not necessarily translate into being good at leading others to do that task. Moreover, poor communication skills on the part of people in leadership creates problems that go beyond limiting one's own career aspirations. Poor communication on the part of leaders hinder an organization's ability to create alignment across levels and departments, to run effectively, and to implement its strategies. Poor communication skills sabotage organizational effectiveness by leading employees to become disengaged, cynical, and unproductive. In extreme cases, poor communication has had life or death consequences.

In all likelihood you are reading this book now because people have identified you as having "what it takes" to be a leader. Perhaps you have risen to the top of your technical field. Perhaps others naturally like and respect you and are drawn to follow you. Or perhaps you have a natural feel for how to create and sustain lasting interpersonal relationships. Some of the most successful people in leadership positions did not seek out those roles—instead, others urged them to take on increasingly visible and important assignments.

Exceptional leaders tend as a rule not to be driven by ambition but rather by a passion for serving others and a desire to accomplish great things. When someone assumes a formal leadership position, they are nearly always at first surprised by how different—and how difficult— the work can be. Managing other people is one of the hardest things a human being can try to do. But why? Because despite the great technological accomplishments of the human race, we remain rank beginners at human relationships and human communication.

Along the same lines, research on effective leadership clearly shows that when leaders stumble, it is rarely due to a lack of technical ability. Instead, they are most challenged by the complexities of relating to others. In this book, we provide you with a comprehensive way of thinking about your own development as a leader focused on three major processes:

- Conducting an honest **self-assessment** focused on your level of self-awareness;

- Clarifying the **choices/decisions** you make regarding your communication and your relationships; and

- Designing and applying a **continuous improvement process** for your leadership and for those you lead.

If you apply the ideas in this book to your own journey, we guarantee that you will see improvements in how others respond to you and in your overall leadership performance.

This book has been written to and for you. It is the result of a close collaboration between its authors (a professor and a practitioner) that has spanned nearly two decades. As a result of our experience in the organizational communication field, we have identified the concepts and behaviors that make the most difference in promoting effective communication. The theories and practices described throughout this book have been road-tested in countless one-on-one coaching sessions and organization-wide initiatives. It is time to share what we have learned so that everyone can reap the benefits of improved communication.

Be aware that these benefits can be quite dramatic. You may see results right away and receive feedback from others that you somehow "seem different"—and in a good way! For now, all that is required is for you to acknowledge that you could do better—and for you to begin to explore how you can improve your communication.

The insights that we offer about communication, while obvious to us because of our work, are unknown to many educated, successful, and technically accomplished people. This is largely due to a persistent (and misguided) tendency to categorize interpersonal effectiveness as a "soft" skill, relegating it to a "nice but not necessary" ability. Professionals in almost every field naively regard communication as something anyone can do, if they would simply put their mind to it. The misunderstood notion persists that as long as a person can talk and hear, then they can speak and listen. Nothing could be further from the truth. This book seeks to dispel this myth once and for all.

These antiquated notions are misleading and destructive. The fact that so many leaders continue to think this way is a big reason why they struggle. Fortunately, there is a growing consensus in even the most technical industries that an inability to express one's ideas orally or in writing, or to work with diverse teams of people are not "soft" but central. Thankfully, one hears the phrase "soft skills" less frequently these days. Like tennis, guitar, or scuba diving, communication is a learned skill that all people can improve upon if they apply themselves. But to improve their communication skills, a person must first see the value of this skill set and recognize that improvement is both possible and desirable.

Playing the guitar is not just plucking strings; it requires complex tuning adjustments and plucking/strumming finger work. Without these efforts, the result could sound more like noise than music.

Communicating is not just talking and listening; it requires complex message displays and engaging the listener followed by an assessment to check for understanding. It is not just throwing words back and forth. Without these efforts, the result could sound more like noise than meaningful dialogue. It's about making the most out of the words you do say. It's time to *stop wasting words* and learn how to truly communicate effectively.

Please be forewarned that at first reading, some of the ideas in this book may seem obvious, confusing, or strange. We encourage you to consider each of them carefully and urge you to be patient. Effective communication is closely linked to effectiveness in many other aspects of life, hence there tends to be a fair amount of defensiveness associated with considering the validity of these concepts (e.g., "That's obvious," or "I already do that!"). At the very least, *before* you decide that a specific concept may not apply to you, you might want to ask someone you know or work with for their opinion—their answer may surprise you.

All of the stories, examples, and solutions contained in this book are true. In order to respect and protect the privacy of our clients, we have changed the names of people and their organizations.

Organization of This Book

Much of the information in this book has been drawn from research on animal and human communication. We will also introduce you to several innovative, new approaches. These new approaches have made a significant difference with leaders in organizations, medical practices, universities, government agencies, Boy and Girl Scout troops, and families. Whatever your own situation, you can use these approaches immediately to communicate more effectively. That said, making changes in one's routine behavior can be difficult. The diet and exercise industries prosper in large part because people try and fail and try again to develop healthier daily routines. Studies of habitual behavior reveal that while it may take only a few hours to learn a new behavior, weeks or months are required to permanently replace that old, unwanted behavior with a new, more desirable one.

What this means is that if you want to grow and develop as a leader, you should *expect* to find it difficult to create lasting changes in your behavior, and you will likely struggle with the reappearance of undesirable behaviors when you become unfocused or stressed.

In our experience, however, this is not the main obstacle to leadership development. Instead, we have observed that many aspiring leaders are simply *unaware of their current communication style and its impact on others.* Consequently, we chose the idea of creating self-awareness—becoming conscious of one's own communication—as the starting point for the book. Self-awareness lays the groundwork for the adoption of new behaviors. This topic is covered in Part One.

Once people have a better understanding of their current communication style, they are ready to more closely examine their specific communication goals in relating to others. Part Two of this book focuses on how to become conscious of one's *intentions* as a means for becoming more strategic in communicating with others. A key theme of this section is that all communication has the potential to accomplish multiple goals. As such, communicative choices always improve when we become more aware of both our actual intentions and our desired impact on others—before we say anything out loud.

Building upon this greater knowledge of one's communication style and intentions, Part Three brings other people into the picture, taking up the subject of feedback: what it is, how to get it, what it means, and how it may be used to further your leadership journey. There are many significant misunderstandings surrounding how feedback works in relationships, and in this section we seek to correct these wrong impressions.

Part Four brings even more people into the picture by extending the idea of conscious communication into the realm of leadership teams and the total organization. Here we focus on the role of the leader in shaping an organizational culture in which people are comfortable fully engaging with others in the service of individual and communal well-being, as well as in overall performance. We return to our original theme of leadership as conscious communication, offering additional examples and advice for your journey toward more conscious communication in teams and in building a more conscious culture and a more effective organization.

We close the book in Part Five with stories from our practice. We offer examples of how conscious communication can improve individual, team, and organizational performance throughout the book, but in this last chapter we also show how the principles of conscious communication can be applied diagnostically. We provide ten client examples in which we demonstrate the application of specific conscious communication principles that enable leaders to create sustainable coaching interventions and results.

Chapter One

We Do Not Know What We Do Not Know

Y ou must start here: *We do not know what we do not know.* Like the first step in a twelve-step recovery program, which asks you to admit that you are powerless and that your life has become unmanageable, *this step is not optional* for those who sincerely wish to improve their communication. The willingness to admit that there are things we do not know about ourselves creates a foundation of humility that is essential for making any lasting improvement. If you are unwilling to entertain the possibility that you may have significant blind spots about yourself, please stop here. However, if you are willing to be humbled as a means for doing better, read on.

All of us experience vast areas of our daily life in which we do not know how things work. Most of us drive a car without knowing the science of the combustion engine. We use electricity, plumbing, computers, and cell phones without knowing how they actually operate. When something goes wrong with these things, many of us may think "I can fix that," or "It can't be that hard to fix this myself."

Such beliefs can have humorous consequences. A friend owns a hair salon. Recently we overheard a phone conversation while getting a haircut. The gist of the call was that someone tried to color her own hair and now, on the morning of a wedding, she needed emergency help. We asked the owner what percentage of her business came from people who thought they could take care of their own needs. She said that nearly 40 percent of her business came from people who did not know what they did not know. There is indeed a reason why people go to school to learn how to do these things!

Another example illustrates the same point. Consider a university board of trustees confronted with the need to better market their school both nationally and globally. When the school's department of marketing presented a professional, comprehensive marketing campaign to the board, one member suggested that instead of doing that work (and spending all that money), they could simply ask a class of undergraduates to develop a marketing plan as a class project. While the students might indeed get a lot out of this experience, the board member's suggestion reflects the tacit belief that communication is something "anyone" can do. This board member would have never suggested that students should redo the architectural master plan, prepare a gourmet dinner, or conduct a financial audit. However, in the realm of communication, many otherwise educated people do not regard it as a learned, professional skill.

Relatedly, many otherwise brilliant individuals can be very poor communicators. While humans have the capacity to be skillful in many domains, communication is generally not one of them; regardless of intelligence or experience, we are *all* mostly beginners at human relationships. If you need convincing on this point, pick up the biography of any accomplished leader to witness the relational carnage that typically accompanies their success. These personal struggles are especially frustrating for people who are bright and accustomed to figuring things out, when they learn that they do not have the same level of insight or success in their ability to relate to others.

While intelligent people sense they *ought* to know how to communicate well, in reality they may fail to achieve the outcomes they desire. Many prefer to blame others rather than consider their own contribution to communication failures. If we do not know what we do not know, we are helpless to improve our skills. In this respect, knowledge of "how to communicate effectively" falls into a surprising category, more like nutrition or spiritual practice than grammar or math; success has less to do with conceptual understanding and more to do with committed, repeated, disciplined practice. In this way, learning about communication is like learning about death; while we know it is inevitable, most of us resist learning too much about it and would prefer to just let it happen to us (but not too soon!). Unfortunately, many organizations are willing to forgive and even enable poor communicators whom they perceive as contributing in other important ways.

Worse yet, as consultants we all too often observe poor communicators who feel confident and even proud of their (woeful) communication skills! We suppose that this is an easy conclusion to reach when one has little interest in examining one's impact on others. Circular reasoning and self-sealing rationalization can easily outweigh any effort to objectively validate one's skills. Something like this: "I am always right because I believe I am always right. Any problems I have must therefore be other people's fault."

Unfortunately—and in our view, somewhat shockingly—most communication theory, teaching, consulting, and training ignore *all* of these points and instead begin with the notion that most people already have (1) an understanding of the importance of communication to leadership success and (2) a clear picture of their own inter-personal strengths and weaknesses, talents and blind spots. *Nothing could be further from the truth.* In working with most leaders, we often remind them that if they are unaware of their own weaknesses, they are likely the only ones in their organization who are.

By contrast, every exceptional leader we have ever met is keenly aware of what they don't know; moreover, they purposefully surround themselves with others who already have that knowledge or perspective. The key to beginning the leadership journey is to *conduct an honest self-assessment* of your approach to communication and relationships, the goal of which is to gather information about what you don't know about yourself.

Moreover, many current communication training programs for leaders neglect the fundamentals and focus disproportionately on advanced skills. In so doing, they send a message that the practitioners in these programs have already mastered the basics, while in reality very often they unequivocally have not. We believe that a return to these fundamentals is required and will dramatically improve your ability to have a positive impact on communication practice.

A story illustrates how impervious we can be to our own com-munication abilities (or lack thereof). At a summer campfire among some friends, Bill shared a personal story about how difficult and incompetent *all* the town department employees were. He had spent about a week attempting to conduct business with people from the highway department, fire department, cemetery commission, parks and recreation, and school departments. He concluded that they were *all* rude and obnoxious and that "everyone had an attitude problem." He further speculated that all town employees were grossly incom-petent and most likely derived pleasure from giving the taxpayers of the town a hard time.

But a different pattern was obvious to every other person around the campfire. The common denominator among all these diverse interactions was Bill himself! Yet Bill had no clue that his own behavior was the likely cause of most of his troubles with other people. (He also had no reason to even suspect that his own behavior was the problem, because he had already concluded that everyone else was an idiot.) As long as he had settled on a plausible theory, he had no reason to look any further. The thought, "Gee, I wonder if I am contributing to this," had never occurred to him, just as it so very rarely occurs to any of us.

Family therapist John Bradshaw reveals a similar insight in his description of an angry Houston driver, Joe, looking for a parking space at a shopping mall during the holidays. Joe became frustrated and subsequently belittled another driver he saw who was relaxed, smiling at other cars, and waving people ahead of her. Meanwhile, Joe became increasingly angry at all the other drivers who would not stop to make a space for him. But it never occurred to him that by his own behavior of scowling and cursing, Joe himself was in fact *creating* the very negative reactions that he was so quick to attribute to the offensive and seemingly hostile intent of others.

A willingness to get to know oneself better is the first and most important step on the leadership journey.

A willingness to get to know oneself better is the first and most important step on the leadership journey. Put differently, in order to grow, leaders must learn to empty their cup. "Empty your cup" is an old Chinese Chan (Zen) saying that is occasionally featured in Western popular media. It is often attributed to a conversation between the scholar Tokusan (also called Te-shan Hsuan-chien, 782–865) and Zen Master Ryutan (Lung-t'an Ch'ung-hsin or Longtan Chongxin, 760–840).

Scholar Tokusan, who was full of knowledge and opinions about the dharma, came to Ryutan and asked about Zen. At one point Ryutan refilled his guest's teacup but did not stop pouring when the cup was full. Tea spilled out and ran over the table. "Stop! The cup is full!" said Tokusan.

"Exactly," said Master Ryutan. "You are like this cup; you are full of ideas. You come and ask for teaching, but your cup is full; I can't put anything in. Before I can teach you, you'll have to empty your cup."

Emptying one's cup is difficult, especially for people raised and educated in the Western hemisphere, where individuality and rationality are generally favored over empathy and emotion. From a young age, children are taught to "stand up" for what they believe, so much so that Americans in particular almost inevitably translate any difference in perspective into an opposition (i.e., I'm right, therefore you must be wrong). We live in what sociolinguist Deborah Tannen calls an "argument culture," where constructive dialogue is rarely encouraged and at times belittled.

If current political events have taught us anything, it is that there remains a deep reluctance on the part of most adults to look critically at their own worldview or to make themselves vulnerable to others' perspectives. This difficulty is important because self-knowledge and the ability to appreciate others' points of view is *the essential leadership capability*. While a leader may be strong in every other way, if they struggle with understanding the perspectives of their peers, employees, customers, or various other stakeholders, *they will fail*. Getting out of and over oneself begins, however, with getting *into* oneself, by developing a detailed understanding of one's own perspective and world view.

In summary, if a leader's sense of self prevents him/her from accepting the fact that he or she might not know everything, then he or she will never succeed. To learn what we do not know, we must swallow our pride, consider that we do not know everything, and begin to look at ourselves from the world's perspective, not our own "I am perfect" perspective. Only then can we become effective leaders.

Emptying one's cup means taking responsibility for the role each of us plays in shaping all of our relationships. It requires us to do something that at first seems quite difficult—to imagine how we appear to other people. Try this thought experiment: How do the people closest to you describe you when you are not around? What do others feel are your greatest strengths? What do they feel are your greatest weaknesses? When do they find you to be just plain annoying? Chances are that you have rarely, if ever, asked yourself these kinds of questions, and even reading them here may be making you nervous about the probable answers! While this kind of feedback can indeed be hard to hear, soliciting and being open to hearing it is key to growing and developing successfully as a leader.

Human awareness is a complex thing. We are called upon to do so many different things each day that much of what we know gets placed into what has been called "practical" or "tacit" knowledge. This is information that allows us to behave competently without conscious awareness of how we are doing so. It is easy to see how this works with regard to breathing or circulating our blood, but it also applies to our morning routines and driving our cars; and can creep into many of our daily work activities. It is sometimes called muscle memory. (Have you ever driven somewhere and upon arrival realize that you don't remember anything about the trip?) According to psychologist Ellen Langer, much of the time, we behave "mindlessly" in accordance with long-established patterns and tacit, unspoken knowledge. This is generally a good thing because it allows us to lead rich, varied, and complex lives that are not limited by our capacity for conscious self-awareness or choice.

Sometimes, however, practical knowledge can keep us mired in patterns that are destructive or limiting. This happens because *unless and until* you bring a pattern into consciousness (i.e., translate it into what is sometimes called "discursive knowledge"), *you cannot change it.* This is why getting feedback about how you appear to others is so important; it moves knowledge about your behavior from the practical realm into the discursive realm, making it open to scrutiny and to change. This is similar to what we all appreciate to be true about "sacred cows" or "elephants in the room"; so long as their existence remains unspoken, they retain their power and are likely to persist. Once seen and identified, lasting change becomes possible.

Consider a meeting among business partners who have known each other for decades at an office party. One person will innocently say, "Yeah, you always beat a dead horse until we agree with you, but it's OK because we're used to it." Everyone in the room will nod in agreement. The second person will respond, "No way, I don't do that." At this point, that person may resist and argue. Or that person can let go of this aspect of self-concept, empty his or her cup, and say, "I never knew I came across this way. I need to be aware of this behavior. Thank you for letting me in on it!"

Along these lines, there are two questions we routinely ask of leaders when they request our help in promoting communication and positive change in their organizations. The first has to do with changing a dysfunctional corporate culture. When asked how we might help to create a more positive culture, we stop them and turn the question around—how do you and your employees come to work every day and perpetuate the dysfunctional culture? This question can be jarring but prompts people to look directly at the role they play in creating and sustaining the status quo (whether they claim to like it or not).

The second question has to do with how leaders listen. We challenge leaders to answer the question "How are you already listening?" which at first may seem like an odd turn of a phrase. What we are trying to do here is get at leaders' typical listening stance before they even know who is speaking or what that person is speaking about. After some confusion and resistance (often in the form of "I listen differently in every situation," which cannot be true), there is a growing awareness of personal listening patterns. Typical answers can be "I listen to solve problems," or "I listen to protect myself politically." Once again, simply becoming aware of one's usual listening stance brings it into the discursive realm, making it available for change.

When people are chosen for leadership roles, it is because they have been successful in some aspect of their work. They are understandably motivated to repeat this success as a leader, which often leads to defensiveness and tunnel vision and a tendency to see all problems and challenges as external to themselves. In struggling to implement a new project, their leadership inexperience may cause them to fault others for being uncooperative. They may also fault senior leadership for not understanding and/or supporting the value of what they bring to the table. While both of these things could be true, these external challenges are usually easier to entertain than a very different kind of inquiry: introspective questions such as "What am *I* doing to contribute to the current predicament, and what might I do differently?" and "What can I learn from what is happening here?"

Unfortunately, the bias toward not taking responsibility for one's communication as a leader is widespread. Many years ago, we worked with an engineer who had risen to the position of general manager at a major defense contractor in California. Several months later he had received increased complaints from customers about quality; his response was to develop a quality communication campaign complete with a new slogan, posters, buttons, and an airplane flying over the plant dropping leaflets that said, "Satisfy the customer with first-time quality." Weeks later, the quality situation had not improved, and the general manager was perplexed. He had told the employees what to do. Why hadn't they listened? The possibility that did not even enter his mind was the simple question: "Was this the best way for me to engage my employees in encouraging them to deliver better quality?"

Contrast that defensive reaction with this alternative approach taken recently by a VP of strategy in a large New England healthcare system. In an unusually emotional meeting, a number of people on the team were expressing their concerns to the CEO regarding members saying negative things about senior leaders on the team to others in the organization. This VP sat quietly and listened for a long time until finally the CEO asked her what she was thinking. She said that she was listening very hard as a means for reflecting on her own behavior outside of meetings, to determine whether any of her own communicative choices could have been seen as undermining to her teammates. She added further that she had indeed said some things to her direct reports in the spirit of open communication that she now realized were inappropriate; she apologized to her colleagues and pledged to not repeat these practices in the future.

This type of self-examination response is the gold standard of communication, but it is exceedingly rare. More often, we see executives who blame their employees for not performing, when the bigger problem is that the executives themselves have not set clear direction and expectations. Similarly, when a business leader tells her directors and managers what they need to do and later discovers that the employees are not following this direction, the business leader quite often misunderstands the cause. This leader will send their directors and managers to leadership development programs to learn to listen better, will order their directors to create more accountability in their respective areas, and will complain that the HR department is failing to hire capable employees. All of these actions point to issues outside of the business leader. As such, none of these actions get to the real problem, which lies with the leader.

We hardly ever hear a leader say, "I wonder if there is something in the way that I am communicating my priorities that is making my communication less effective than it could be." In his powerful book *The Flight of the Buffalo: Confessions of a Recovering Autocrat*, James D'Alessandro traces his personal transformation as a leader to one powerful insight—that by telling people what to do, he was depriving his employees of the opportunity to learn and to grow. With that recognition in mind, it became obvious to him not only *how*, but also *why* he needed to change his communication as a leader, to be less controlling, and to be more open to alternative ways of doing things.

One final example, also drawn from health care, reveals a similar dynamic. When a physician saw that a patient who had been discharged only a week ago had just been readmitted to the hospital (a very costly outcome), her first impulses were to believe that the patient was not following discharge instructions, was not taking the prescribed medications, or was noncompliant in some other way. By contrast, a physician who is more self-reflective about their own communication, upon seeing such a readmission, might think or say the following:

- I wonder if I missed part of the underlying problem.

- I wonder if my patient was given all the instructions that they needed at discharge and was actually shown how to use the at-home medical devices.

- I wonder if we could have done something different or better to support this patient when he was sent home.

In summary: Effective leadership depends on effective communication, and the first step to becoming a more effective communicator is to develop a deeper understanding of how you are *already* communicating. There are a number of "official" methods for getting this information; organizations often collect this data as part of 360-degree performance evaluations. An even better method is to actively approach the people you work with and to repeatedly and sincerely ask them to share their perceptions of your own leadership actions with you.

The first time you ask for this type of feedback, everyone will be cautious until they determine if you really want to hear it. You will most certainly have to ask a few times before anyone will share their honest perception of you. In addition, you will be *more* successful soliciting feedback if you are specific in your request: Asking "how could I have run that meeting better" will likely yield more useful information than a vague "how am I doing." Finally, soliciting honest feedback is about creating a "virtuous" (as opposed to vicious) cycle. When feedback is offered to you, the person who gave it will watch carefully to see (1) if there are any negative consequences because of it; and (2) if you do anything positive with it. If there are no negative consequences, and if you do something positive, then there is a strong likelihood you will receive further feedback in the future. We will talk much more about the power of feedback in Chapter Six.

In the meantime, we encourage you to experiment with the explanations that you develop when things become difficult for you. The main insight advanced by many psychotherapy and recovery programs is that all change begins with oneself, and that acting the same way and expecting different results is insane. Rather than defaulting to how the actions of others are creating obstacles, begin by considering what *you* could do differently. Of course, in some cases the problem really will lie with others; however, there are tremendous advantages to examining one's own behavior first.

CHAPTER TWO

The Receiver of the Message Assigns Its Meaning

Most people think that the sender of a message controls its meaning, leading to the (often) false assumption that receivers will automatically interpret one's communication in the way that it was intended. To the contrary, the fundamental yet revolutionary idea that the receiver assigns the meaning of a message can take weeks, months, or even a lifetime for some people to understand and to accept. While it is perhaps the most basic concept in modern communication theory, most people have never had the opportunity to formally study communication and, therefore, have had to learn it by trial and error, often surrounded by other people who also lack this training.

To illustrate this principle, consider a true story about a vice president in a billion-dollar organization who was sincerely interested in improving both employee satisfaction and workforce productivity. He had taken workshops on the subject of employee engagement and came away with the idea that he could better engage his subordinates by sharing personal stories. The workshop presenters intended their participants to learn the value of sharing *relatable* stories about, for example: pets, flat tires, and kids at home not wanting to do chores. This vice president reflected on this lesson for a few weeks and decided to share a personal story at his next staff meeting.

Since he had never done this before, he felt anxious about taking such a bold step and contacted us a few days before his staff meeting. He told us about his intention to use personal storytelling to build rapport with employees. He went on to tell us that he planned to show slides (that he had taken with his new $4,000 camera) of his family enjoying themselves at an exclusive international resort. He reasoned that because most people take pictures of their vacations, this would be an ideal story. His second story was about boating. He had recently purchased a forty-five-foot sailboat and was looking forward to sailing up and down the east coast of the US on his next vacation.

How do you suppose such stories would be received by a room full of hourly employees, many of whom use their vacation time to work extra jobs to provide for their families? Without exception, the receiver decides the meaning of the message. The employees, if attentive, might have been able to quote various parts of his story, up to and including the length of his new boat! However, the meaning they would have assigned to this person would likely not have been, "I feel so engaged. I can relate to those stories. I am so glad that our vice president is a regular kind of person. Our leader really cares for us and values our work." Rather, a more likely interpretation would be the following: "How can this guy be so out of touch? If he can afford a forty-five-foot sailboat, he should be paying us more. What a narcissist, coming here and bragging about what he does with his family. He really must not care about us at all."

Despite our best wishes and intentions, the meaning of what we say is *always* assigned by the receiver. In order to act consciously with this information, leaders must abandon the most pervasive misconception about communication: the belief that it is somehow possible to "transmit" information from one person's brain to another. Decades ago, communication researchers debunked this "conduit" metaphor of communication, yet it persists out of a desire by many otherwise smart people to see human communication as somehow akin to information engineering. In plain fact, *interpretation always trumps intent*. Receivers assign meaning based upon what you say, how you say it, and their own lifetime of experiences that shape their perceptions. Against this backdrop, your intended meaning simply does not matter.

A disconnect between one's intended meaning and how one is interpreted occurs across multiple contexts, both within and outside of the workplace. A majority of family arguments contain the phrase, "But that's not what I meant!" We can all become frustrated when a receiver's interpretation of our communication differs dramatically from what we intended. When this occurs, nearly everyone who has not learned this principle quickly looks to blame the other individual for missing the point, misinterpreting the message, or having a bias. But there is no use in blaming or arguing—like they say in the advertising field, in the final analysis "perception is reality," and we must start there. Arguing over how others *should have* interpreted your meaning is a fruitless and losing battle. While information may be transmitted orally or electronically, the meaning of that information is entirely dependent upon the vocabulary, experiences, and emotional state of the person receiving it. For example: I may criticize your performance in an attempt to "light a fire" under you, but you may hear such criticism as blaming and even belittling.

All too often, when leaders talk about "improving" their communication with others, the end result is "canned" messages either via email or in person through PowerPoint presentations, which rarely have the desired effect. This is because paramount in the mind of the receiver—and crucial to their interpretation of the "canned" message—is their own perception of you as a person and of the nature of the relationship that they feel they have with you. If you are perceived as an authentic and caring person, as someone who genuinely values employees as human beings equal to yourself, then nearly any message from you will be heard favorably. But if they see you or have experienced you to be cold and insincere, appearing to create distance and separation between yourself and others, then no amount of positive messaging will make a difference. In the realm of teaching, this is sometimes expressed as "they will not care to know until they know you care."

Another powerful example of the importance of relationships in shaping how meaning is assigned has to do with messages sent and received during shift changes in hospitals. When a new shift reports to work, physicians and nurses "hand off" critical information concerning the existing patients to the incoming professionals to ensure continuity of care. In health care, researchers and the hospital accrediting body all recognize that this is a vulnerable process for patient safety, as valuable information may be lost or misconstrued. Unfortunately, most of the guidelines and regulations that have been applied to improve this critical process take an outdated information transmission approach. Incoming staff are encouraged to repeat back what they have been told, and outgoing staff are encouraged to put all continuing orders in writing. While these changes can help to a degree, the quality of the handoff ultimately depends on the quality of the relationship between the participants. Do they trust each other?

Do they take the time to put their observations in context, or do they rush through the process in a series of one-way messages? Are they willing and able to discuss and ask questions about what they don't know about the patients? Is the communication climate one of respect and appreciation for each other's contributions? If not, a psychologically unsafe environment can contribute to a person's fear of looking bad trumping the employee's feeling safe enough to raise a concern about confusing medical orders or patient safety.

A poignant example of how meaning works in relationships can be found in the seemingly simple phrase, "I love you!" At some point in our lives, we all say this to someone. Sometimes someone says these three words to us. Imagine the meaning of these three simple words when expressed by and to the following people:

PERSON SPEAKING	WORDS SPOKEN	PERSON BEING SPOKEN TO
Father putting child to bed at night	*I love you!*	2-year-old child
Mother dropping off child at day care in order to go to work	*I love you!*	2-year-old child
43-year-old husband, married for 11 years	*I love you!*	27-year-old secret girlfriend
Grandfather taking his grandson fishing	*I love you!*	10-year-old grandson
Great-grandmother in hospice trying to convey a lifetime of love	*I love you!*	5-year-old great granddaughter
25-year-old male proposing marriage	*I love you!*	17-year-old high school student he wants to marry
3-year-old daughter who wants to stay up late rather than go to bed	*I love you!*	Mother who needs child to go to sleep in order to do the laundry
8-year-old son	*I love you!*	Father who is bringing his son back home after weekend visitation
3-year-old daughter who is hugging mom's neck so tight she does not want to let go	*I love you!*	Mother who is trying to drop her daughter off at day care, so she can go to work
57-year-old adult after finding out his partner needs a life-threatening/saving operation	*I love you!*	Life partner who feels very frightened.

The meaning of the words "I love you" (and indeed, of any phrase) is fully dependent upon the context and the meaning of these words *to the receiver*. In fact, the phrase can even have multiple meanings at the same time! The person expressing this message has an idea or emotion that he or she wishes to convey. By using tone, volume, gestures, eye contact, and facial expressions, the speaker utters these words. The sound of the words travels through the air. If the receiver's hearing is not compromised in any way, for example, from a head cold, background noise, anxiety, or some other sort of interference, then the sound reaches the receiver. In the case of a face-to-face exchange, the receiver likely also has his or her eyes open and can see facial gestures. For example, is the speaker making eye contact or looking away? The meaning assigned to eye contact varies across cultures and is always part of the message. A variety of clarifying questions can shape the interpretation. Are the words spoken sincerely or superficially? Were they expressed passionately or routinely? Did the individual speak softly or loudly, each of which could affect interpretation?

The person being spoken to hears the sound of the words, sees the expression of the speaker, and comes to a conclusion about what has been conveyed. *The meaning of these words is assigned by the receiver.* This meaning may or may not be the same as that which is intended, and this is very often where communication challenges arise. Multiple factors in the communicative context—such as time, place, others who are present—can affect sense-making. A wise individual once said that perhaps the greatest threat to communication is the mistaken belief that it has occurred.

> **Perhaps the greatest threat to communication is the mistaken belief that it has occurred.**

Unfortunately, a related myth—that the communicator can somehow *control* the meaning of communication—is deeply ingrained in most leaders. This erroneous assumption manifests itself in mandatory training programs, top-down strategy sessions, and all types of cascading messaging and program "rollouts"—forcing a message to flow from the top down to every level of the corporate structure, like a waterfall. As communication experts, our advice to all leaders is as follows: Please abandon the idea of any kind of rollout altogether. Through communication, we can invite people to give their attention to our messages, we can believe we have enrolled them into our vision, but we absolutely cannot control their interpretation.

Formal program rollouts almost always result in vast numbers of employees *pretending* to get the message, then questioning the value of these communications behind the scenes. For leaders, top-down rollouts are tempting because they allow you to "check a box" allowing for the appearance that something has been communicated, whether that something is a new strategy, a financial update, or a new diversity policy. By now we hope we have made it clear that simply delivering a message means nothing by itself—the receiver controls the interpretation and assigns the meaning.

Practically speaking, what this means is that exceptional leaders need to plan their communication in ways that begin with anticipating the likely audience response, then following up by checking how the message was in fact received. Experienced leaders develop a detailed sense of what mechanisms of communication work best both for their messages to reach their employees (e.g., town halls vs. webcasts) and for monitoring the degree to which the meaning assigned by the audience matches the leaders' intended meaning. Those leaders then vary their approaches to accommodate different perceptions and preferences. If you begin with an analysis of how an audience will likely react to a message, and if you have a strategy to find out what the message means to a majority of the employees, then there is a greater likelihood that you will make the appropriate communicative choices.

When one begins with the question "How will my communication likely be received?"—the answer suggests many possible courses of action. Research on persuasion suggests that if you anticipate specific objections an audience may have to your message, it is wise to include these objections early in the message and to refute them, concluding with a desired proposal, call to action, or recommendation. When this order is reversed, that is if a message begins with a proposal and toward the end of the message the leader acknowledges some people's reservations or objections, audiences tend to see the leader as defensive or hostile. The more conscious a leader is of the desired results/outcomes of a message, the key ingredients of the message, the options available for delivering the message, and the meaning most likely to be assigned to the message by the audience (regardless of the leader's intent), the better able the leader is to present a credible and coherent point of view more likely to be given the same meaning by the audience as is intended by the leader.

If you strive to be a better communicator (and if you have come this far in the book, we are convinced that you do!), we recommend that you once and for all disavow yourself of a number of widely held myths about communication.

THREE MYTHS

Meaning is transmitted from person to person.

Not so. Human communication is unequivocally not a transmission process; rather, the sender chooses words believed to match his/her intent, which are open to the receiver's interpretation and assigning of meaning based upon that person's (or their) perception and personal experiences.

Words have meaning.

A close cousin of the first myth, this is also false. It is tempting to believe that if you can just find the correct words, then you will be understood. In fact, the meaning of all words varies across receivers, and their meanings, therefore, lie more in the minds of the people doing the interpretation than in the words themselves.

The clearer the communication the better.

Also false. Communication can be used to accomplish multiple, at times conflicting goals, and clarity is not the sole indicator of effectiveness. In an ideal world, clear words would result in a clear message. But we already know that words have multiple meanings, so clarity is an unattainable goal. Clarity to the leader is not always clarity for the employee. For example, leaders must often be tactful or purposefully ambiguous to preserve employee self-esteem or avoid political fallout. There are many times when clear, open communication is not the best choice for the situation.

A belief in any one of these myths compromises communication effectiveness. One of us has the privilege of working in university administration, where department chairs are called upon to motivate faculty to improve their teaching and research efforts. By all accounts, these chairs are among the brightest individuals one could ever hope to meet. But as we have observed, technical brilliance is not a reliable predictor of leadership effectiveness. All too often, people taking on these roles try to establish direction rationally and autocratically, focusing on the reasonableness (to themselves!) of their own vision and goals. They genuinely believe the meaning of their messages are self-evident and will often make reference to other messages they have delivered as they attempt to "add clarity." They send out messages in the forms of emails, proposals, white papers, and PowerPoint slide decks, expending great efforts to make sure their messages, slides, and graphics are clear. Such efforts start at the wrong end of the communication process. Successful academic leaders must first learn as much as they can about the faculty and staff they wish to influence. Only then can they begin to craft a vision that these potential followers will find compelling.

A recent campus interview of a candidate for the position of Business School Dean illustrates this difference very well. When the candidate was asked about his vision for transforming the College of Business, he paused and said that while he had some general ideas, he would much prefer to "hit the ground listening." He got the job, listened for a year, and is now beginning to introduce strategic goals that have the support of his faculty. Just as there is no meaning without interpretation, there can be no leadership without followers.

We once gave a physician client this perspective about meaning being assigned by the receiver:

> Imagine that your patients all have their own definitions, their own dictionaries. Their name is on the cover, not Webster's. Every word in their dictionary has a meaning which has been influenced by their unique life experiences. Some of the words in their dictionary have a fairly common meaning within their household or family—the words they use for meals, soda pop,

or desserts. Other words they use may apply to work habits or chores. A musically talented family we know has found that a lot of music terms mean things to them that are different than nonmusical families—words like harmony, teamwork, and practice.

As a result, if I say something to you and you "misunderstand" me or "misinterpret" what I am trying to say, from our perspective, there is actually no "miss." You have not failed to see my words from my point of view. You have not failed to listen carefully to me. You are, quite simply, working with a different dictionary. And I am in no position to scold you for not using my dictionary because you do not have access to my personal dictionary. Quite practically, if I have something important to share with you, I need to attend to the meaning you assign to my words based upon your personal dictionary. If I care about you, I can do no less. Since many words share a relatively common meaning in all our dictionaries, we easily begin making assumptions that all of the meanings you have for words are identical to mine, something that is simply not true.

The following is Dr. Michael P.'s story:

I was meeting with a woman whose husband was diagnosed with stage four cancer. We had been talking about the disease progression, and I began telling her about our hospice services. She did not want to talk about hospice. She responded by explaining there was going to be a big family reunion in about eleven months, and she was curious to know how much I thought he would be able to be involved in planning it. Then in the following year, they were having a special anniversary, and she wondered if I thought he might still be able to dance to their favorite songs. At this point in the conversation I was fearful she was having some kind of mental split with reality, perhaps denial or even worse. I began thinking about getting psychological or social work support for her. I began to worry about her needs even to the point of no longer talking about her husband's needs.

Then I remembered the lesson about words and their meanings. I reflected on the idea that she is operating with her own dictionary. I told her that I needed to take a moment and check in with her about some of the things we had talked about because many times we physicians use jargon that may not make sense to our patients. I asked her questions about her husband's medical situation, about hospice, about cancer, etc., and all her answers were on target. Then I asked her what "stage four" meant to her, and I will never forget her reply. She said, "Well, four out of ten is not that bad."

I had made an assumption that we shared the same meaning of "stage four." I apologized to her about not having been clear—even though I had thought that I had been clear. I may have even said there are only four stages of cancer. But whatever I had said was beside the point; perhaps my memory was in error. Perhaps she was experiencing some denial, and she did not want to hear that information. In any event, in her dictionary, fourth stage meant four out of ten. After spending only a little bit of time updating her on the four stages of cancer, she was 100 percent with me and fully able to participate in her husband's end-of-life planning.

There is a famous experiment that was conducted with married couples to study how they communicate when under stress. Each member of the couple was asked to sit on opposite sides of a large screen that permitted them to hear but not see each other. Each individual was then given a physical road atlas and asked to work with their spouse to identify the best route from one small city to another on the map.

For half of the couples in the experiment, each member of the pair was given the identical map, and consequently the task was fairly straightforward. For the remainder of the couples, one member of the couple was given a slightly altered map that omitted a few small key streets along the potential route. Unsurprisingly, the route-planning conversations among these couples got off track pretty quickly, as couples became frustrated with one another when told that the road to take was "not there." In a very few cases, couples realized that they had different maps. This provided a breakthrough that allowed them to agree on a route. In most cases, they assumed that they were looking at the same map (they were not), and they never explored their assumptions. This led to anger and confusion.

In summary, if you are trying to improve your communication with others, it is important to consider the following:

- how they have received you in the past

- what they think of you as a communicator

- how they have interpreted key messages that you have tried to deliver, and

- what key words mean to them according to their own personal dictionaries.

Armed with this knowledge, you will be in a much better position to make improvements and to become more effective.

CHAPTER THREE

The Power of the Pause

I f you have houseplants, then you have seen firsthand how they bend toward sunlight. Depending upon the window view and the exposure, plants can cover a considerable distance as they stretch to follow the sun. Plants are genetically programmed in this way—in other words, they cannot choose not to do so. If a plant is not watered on its regular schedule, the leaves will droop and eventually wither. Once watered, they usually come back to life. No plant can exercise the will to pretend to be healthy when deprived of water. Plants have evolved in diverse environments. They have developed water-capture tools (root structures, leaves, needles or thorns) to maximize their survival and reproduction. If a plant is taken out of its natural environment and placed into a different environment, no amount of talking or reasoning will enable the plant to adapt and survive. In other words, plants are hardwired into their stimulus-response environment.

For most animals, when a stimulus is present, their response also follows automatically. Unlike plants, animal mobility enables them to survive a greater distance from food and water. At the same time, they are compelled to pursue what they need to survive. When a mouse is hungry, it will search for food. When it finds cheese, it is incapable of pausing to consider if the cheese is attached to some kind of a trap. It is unable to have a conversation with its friends to discuss options. It simply responds the same way it does to all food: It eats the cheese. Most animals live in a stimulus-response world.

Formerly wild animals that have been domesticated can appear to have moved beyond the stimulus-response world, but this may be a dangerous illusion. I (Sean) worked for a veterinarian one year while working my way through college. One of the animals I took care of was a beautiful lynx. The relatively small wildcat had been kept as a pet but had grown to be too risky to keep at home. The veterinarian's instructions were clear and were not to be modified: Feed the lynx last, only after taking care of all the other animals that were being boarded. Feed him chicken necks by placing this food into his cage with long tongs. Under no circumstances should you feed the animal by hand or pet him. As affectionate as he appeared, he had no capacity to differentiate between chicken necks and human fingers. The lynx lives in a stimulus-response world. If he is hungry, and if he can detect the slightest scent of chicken, then he will move to eat the food, even if it meant eating a chunk of the caregiver's hand along with it.

Fully domesticated animals like dogs and cats also live mostly in a stimulus-response world, albeit somewhat modified by humans. Dogs respond honestly to their owners' behavior, not their owner's intentions. We have known many dog trainers, one of whom told us stories of humans who misunderstood that nature of dogs. One told us about a dog owner who had complained that his dog was inherently shy and timid, and that this condition was getting worse. In truth, the owner was constantly reprimanding the dog and swatting at the animal's face. Another owner had been frustrated that her dog would not come when called, so she angrily chased after the dog and eventually baited him to return with a variety of snacks. Then, as soon as the dog was within reach, she hit the dog with his leash. When asked why, she explained she was reprimanding the dog for not coming. Yet another owner was puzzled that her dog would never listen. It took only a brief conversation and a few minutes of observation to discover that rather than saying, "Fido, come," this owner would say, "Come on over here, go to the kitchen, come out of the bedroom, it's supper time, time to get your medicine." The owner expected her dog to have a functioning vocabulary comparable to that of a young child. The dog was doing the best he could with inconsistent communication from his owner. Animals do not have the capacity to reason about or to question their stimulus-response environment. Additionally, most animal trainers will tell you that what may first appear to be an animal problem usually ends up being an owner problem, and more specifically, an owner communication problem.

But what about human animals? When an employee is having difficulty with a project and goes to her supervisor for assistance, that employee is still subject to stimulus-response reactions. If the supervisor says, "What's the matter with you? I thought you could handle this simple project. Why didn't you come to me sooner?" then that employee may experience a fear of being judged in a hostile manner. Hostility, as a stimulus, can trigger a "fight or flight" reaction. Fighters will argue back about the assignment, defend themselves, and possibly even attack back with, "If you had given better instructions, then I would have been able to get this done on time…" Those who prefer flight will quickly apologize and perhaps never again ask a boss for assistance. They will do everything possible to ask other people for advice. Their goal is to avoid setting themselves up for more hostility.

Perhaps one of their primary goals is "to fly below the radar."

When an employee, be she a dishwasher, supervisor, manager, director, or vice president, is asked to "come to the boss's office," past experience may likely create an anxious situation triggering apprehension: "Am I in trouble? What did I do wrong?" The stimulus is an invitation with no information about the purpose of the meeting, therefore, it must be bad. The response is typically fear or anxiety. Such an employee might enter the boss's office, asking, "Why do you want to see me?" This question, an essentially innocent yet hostile one, can become the stimulus for the boss to say, "Why are you speaking to me in that tone?" From there, things often escalate. Each person's behavior can become a stimulus for the next person's behavior. When we say that we have trouble "getting along" with a coworker or boss, what we are really describing is an enduring pattern of stimulus and response where each party sees the other as being hostile or unhelpful. Over time, these knee-jerk reactions become amplified and difficult to resist, as they now represent a pattern of multiple stimuli each of which are seen as requiring a particular reaction.

But humans differ from other animals in one important way. Humans are the only animals with the capacity to pause after experiencing the stimulus. During this pause, a person can consider options and decide how to respond. In order to do so, we must first become aware of the stimulus-response patterns in which we are participating, particularly those that have become automatic. By moving these patterns from practical to discursive consciousness, change becomes possible. By changing stimulus-response to stimulus-pause-response, we can better consider our options, enabling the opportunity for more effective communication. We are no longer sentenced to endlessly repeat our habitual (and very often counterproductive) reactions.

A client was referred to us by an executive at a Boston hospital.

The client, a nursing leader, had become trapped in a dysfunctional stimulus-response cycle that needed to be understood and disrupted if she were to keep her position. The executive who hired us used the following words to describe the nursing leader's communication: She comes across as "arrogant, always right, and condescending." We were told that when people offered different opinions about her decisions, she yelled at them. While her nursing skills were impeccable, her leadership skills were destructive and reactionary. She acted on what she thought was going on rather than trying to discover what was actually going on in a situation. We were told that if she was unable to change, then they would need to remove her from her role despite her many strengths and clear passion for and advancements in accuracy and quality. The executive wondered: Was there any way to hold on to her expertise but to also "humanize" her interactions with her staff and colleagues?

Fifteen minutes into our first meeting, this client demonstrated clear evidence of the behaviors that had been described to us by her boss. She told me that she had been ordered to see me by a boss who was obviously "out to get her." I asked what the basis of her conclusion was, and she replied that she just knew. She told me she was meeting with me because she was ordered to and that she would always do what she was ordered to do, because she did not want anyone to be able to accuse her of insubordination. She said she was ordered to sit with me for an hour and that was exactly what she planned to do.

But what was really going on here? Referring back to an earlier chapter, she observed her world, came to conclusions about others' intentions, and was reacting in the only way that she felt she could. She was reacting to a perceived threat that was, in our judgment, not real. She angrily believed that people disliked her, when in actuality no one disliked her. She was interpreting her boss's behavior and reacting to protect herself by complying with exactly what she thought she was being told to do. She was aggressively protecting herself. She was fighting back the only way she knew how, except that she was not being attacked. She was trapped in a stimulus-response pattern of perceiving threats that were not real; she was responding by complying with her understanding of precise wording of her leader's orders apparently unconscious of her leader's intentions or her own contributing behavior.

Our view was that many people appreciated her contributions, hoped that she could stop being a bully, wanted her to become more aware of her own behavior, and hoped she would be more effective as a team member. My goal, which became clear in fewer than fifteen minutes, was to help her see that she could pause and choose to become curious instead of reactive, that she could become thoughtful rather than combative. Even as I sat right next to her, she did not see me. She was blinded by the anger of being "sent to see me." I told her that I had different points of view that I would like to explore with her. She replied that she was not interested in speaking with me, that there was nothing wrong with her, and that her intention was to sit at the table for the rest of the hour and then leave.

In an effort to help her to become more conscious of the possibility of an alternative point of view, I decided to share with her that I had received no such orders, i.e., to sit with her for an hour. My assignment was to explore her situation, to examine her satisfaction with her relationships with coworkers, physicians, patients, and to offer ways for her to increase her leadership influence, not her authority to make her staff comply with her commands. She again said that she was not there for any reason other than to comply with her boss's orders to sit with me.

So I tried something else, still hoping to connect with her. I wanted to do something creative, something that would disrupt her rigid thinking. I let her know that it was time for me to leave the room. If I could not work toward accomplishing my goals, which were intended to be helpful, then there was no reason for me to continue. She reiterated that she was instructed to sit with me for an hour, and I reiterated that I had not received the same instructions. I told her that if she wanted to sit with me, then the best I could do was to offer to leave our meeting room and go to my office to get a photograph of myself so that she could sit in the room with that picture. She had meticulously imagined the entire encounter, and this semi-absurd suggestion caught her off guard, penetrating her defensiveness. I was able to see her certainty begin to fade into "What the heck is going on here?" She asked me not to leave. This was the first time she was polite and asked me anything during the encounter.

She went on to inquire about the kind of work I do for leaders. This was the first time she demonstrated curiosity. I offered to show her rather than waste her time telling her stories about other people, and she agreed. I explained to her that one of the things I do is to try to mirror my clients' behaviors so that they can see their own behavior more clearly—so that they can become more conscious of how they appear to others. I then role-played back to her some of her behaviors and nonverbal gestures. She was surprised to see that I could mimic her words and demeanor almost exactly. I asked her how she felt being talked to like that. And so the consult began. She had been unaware that she was trapped in a script that she had created, behaving in response to a threat that did not actually exist. Once she became present with me, she gradually became more conscious of her own communication.

A popular phrase that some people use to justify automatic, typically negative reactions to others is that the other person "pushed my buttons." The idea behind that justification is if I can rationalize that you "made me" angry, you made me upset, you made me late, and you made me make mistakes, then I can continue to believe I am OK. If I lose my temper, then it is not my responsibility and not my fault. It is as though they think, "So long as I am reacting to someone else, I am not responsible for my behavior."

Belief in the justification that others can push our buttons is counterproductive because it suggests that we do not have choices in communication. Taking this way of thinking to its logical conclusion, if we want to feel happy, excited, or joyful, we need to find someone who can push *those* buttons for us. The truth is that while we cannot control other people's communication with us, we can *always* control our responses. Of course, this can be difficult to do in those situations where we have allowed a dysfunctional pattern to develop over time. Change is always possible—we re-create our social worlds every moment of every day. But in order to invoke this change, we must first pause to bring the pattern into discursive consciousness (i.e., become aware of it and make it discussable); we must reflect on the pattern, identify the communication options available, anticipate how our various communication choices may be received, and then make a choice. By becoming accountable for our communication, we lay the essential groundwork for effectively leading others.

Put another way, this is an invitation to first identify and then resist unconscious stimulus-response habits by choosing then building new habits. As we develop the capacity to pause between the stimulus and our response we can begin to thoughtfully explore what we would like to accomplish with our response.

With our many clients, we have found that this pause takes the form of a brief silence, during which we first exhale and inhale before speaking. We are often asked, "What should I be thinking during this pause?" In most cases, constructive thoughts simply do not appear.

If we feel angry about something someone says to us, then the pause space might be filled with frustration, anger, retaliation—none of which are healthy, and none of which will likely advance our goals. If you would like to improve your ability to constructively pause between a stimulus and a response, consider the following true story, which we will follow with a specific list of constructive questions.

A high-level executive with major decision-making responsibility for a service line of an organization became aware of a stimulus-response pattern that was becoming increasingly dangerous for himself, his wife, and their three children. In *his* words, he tended to "overreact" when people "pushed his buttons." More specifically, he explained that he had a very strong reaction when driving and another driver abruptly pulled in front of his car. In reaction to this behavior, he would speed up and tailgate the vehicle for a couple of miles in response to the perceived threat to his family. The executive was aware that he was overreacting, and he knew this was not safe for his family. He added that a version of this problem also showed up at work, and he was worried if he would have to live like this forever.

When we had our first meeting, I asked him to tell me a story about being cut off on the highway again, only much more slowly. I asked him to pause as soon as he began describing the poor driver coming into view alongside of the executive's vehicle. I asked him if this poor driver's behavior was visible in the rearview mirror. He shared that he does not use his rearview mirrors that much. It appeared that he was reacting to a threat; he was startled by this other driver weaving through traffic and cutting him off. We then established as the driver, he could begin to use his rearview mirrors with greater frequency and, therefore, notice poor drivers behind him sooner. This would, at least, reduce the startle reflex. He agreed.

I then asked him to tell me what he was thinking the moment

that the other driver abruptly pulled in front of him. He quickly replied that he was *not* thinking. His response created an opportunity to remind him about the way nonhuman animals respond to stimuli, in contrast to the unique power and opportunity for human beings to pause before responding. We all have a choice—to behave as a nonhuman animal or as a human being. He did not know that he did not know this. He then made the conscious decision to hear how to choose to respond as a human being. We then revisited the question, "What are you thinking when you are cut off?" He gradually became aware of protective feelings; his family was momentarily threatened, describing a real risk at seventy miles per hour. After his buttons were pushed, he felt he had to push back. I advised him that no one had touched him, let alone pushed his buttons, and that in fact he had no buttons to be pushed. I explained that talking about buttons was simply a way of blaming others for his reactions and of avoiding responsibility for his own choices and actions. I introduced the possibility that he could actually go through the experience of being cut off, feel threatened by such actions, and then choose different thoughts and actions. Fortunately, rather than becoming defensive, he then became curious.

I then asked him to tell me who were the most important people to him at the moment he was cut off. He said his wife and children. I asked him how he thought they had perceived his aggressive tailgating response to situations like this. He said that his wife had already told him that she did not like his risky behavior. From the second chapter, we had explored that the receiver decides the meaning of the speaker's communication (words and behavior); as such, he could continually intend to be concerned about his family's safety and they could continually conclude that his behavior was selfish, self-indulgent, adolescent, and disrespectful of their needs. His behavior communicated this to his family, again and again, *despite his intentions*. I then asked him if he thought the driver who cut him off was a competent operator of his vehicle. He said no. I asked him to rationally explain to me his reasoning for choosing to put his family at risk, speeding up to tailgate an incompetent driver. How could this possibly appear to him as a good idea? His response was, "Wow, can I be stupid." I assured him he was not stupid. We then actually worked through the principles we have covered so far in this book:

- He did not know what he did not know.

- He realized the discrepancy between his intent to protect his family, and the contrary message his family assigned to his behavior that appeared to endanger his family.

- He was unaware of the animal stimulus-response reflex, and how he was making unconscious habituated choices.

- He did not know he had the capacity to pause and choose his response.

Once he learned these things, he was immediately able to make better decisions—on the road with his family, and at work.

There are several reflective questions that can help leaders who want to become more conscious of pausing and more effective with their responses. They include but are not limited to the following:

- What is going on here?

- What am I paying attention to, and what else should or could I be paying attention to?

- What appear to be the other person's intentions? (What does that other person desire?)

- What do I want to constructively accomplish? (What outcome do I desire?)

- Which words and behaviors on my part will most likely increase the probability of achieving my goal with the other person?

With over two decades of experience in university administration, we've had the opportunity to work with some of the smartest people on the planet. Despite the presence of high IQs, we remain surprised by how quickly some faculty—and even some department chairs and directors—are willing to send angry and provocative emails in response to perceived problems. Over-the-top, angry emails—also known as "flaming"—can be cathartic to send but never result in positive outcomes. In my work coaching these faculty, I start with a simple question: "What did you think would happen when the person received this?" In every case, the flamer has admitted that they did not think about how their email would be received but instead were preoccupied in how justified they felt about sending it. I have used these moments to teach about the power of the pause—of considering one's short- and long-term goals and the receiver's likely response—and in most every case, I have seen these faculty use greater restraint in the future.

We recognize that we no longer need to blame other people for pushing our buttons. To this day, the executive in this story refers to this consult session as his much needed "buttonectomy."

Progress in learning when and how to pause (to consider our next-step options) is easier to describe than it is to apply. The good news is that all human beings are capable of improving this skill. Once learned, leaders can dramatically improve their communication effectiveness in the board room, the operating room, and the dining room. We recognize that we no longer need to blame other people for pushing our buttons. To this day, the executive in this story refers to this consult session as his much needed "buttonectomy."

The first three chapters of this book have introduced the fundamental ideas underlying conscious communication—the ideas of self-awareness, the fact that the receiver assigns meaning, and the power of the pause. While we will return to these ideas later on, the next part of the book focuses more specifically on ways in which leaders can become more aware of their communicative choices, specifically with regard to their intentions, their language, and the ways in which they can seek feedback from others.

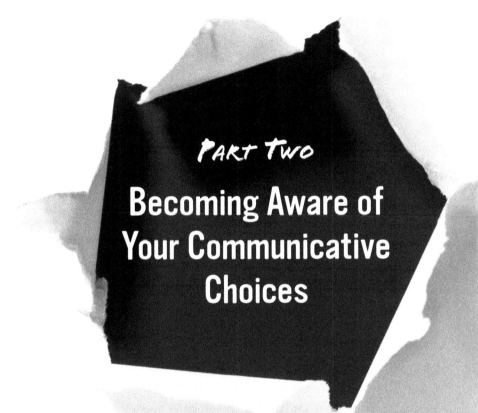

PART TWO

Becoming Aware of Your Communicative Choices

Chapter Four

Communicating with Purpose– Automatic, Expressive, and Conscious Communication

onscious communicators consider their goals and audiences— and potential unanticipated consequences—before they speak or write. They see communication as a powerful tool to be used carefully. They see their communicative acts as more than spontaneous expressions of thoughts or feelings. They see them as strategic choices with varying consequences.

This chapter describes two common communication styles that can be destructive if endorsed by leaders. The first, which we call "automatic," is practiced by leaders who believe that the most important thing in communication is having the *idea*, and that once you have a compelling message in mind, the act of communicating it to others is a nonissue. From this perspective, there is a common expectation that communication is "no big deal" and that once a leader puts a message out there, others will "automatically" get it.

Since we now know from research that this is often not true (the receiver assigns the meaning of the message, see chapter two), it is not surprising that automatics become very frustrated when they are "misunderstood." Moreover, they tend to blame receivers, audiences, and subordinates for not listening carefully enough when such a "misunderstanding" occurs. Most important, since these individuals do not truly understand or value strategic communication (they do not know what they do not know, see chapter one), it never occurs to them that the way they approached the situation could have been improved.

A second common approach to leadership communication is what we call "expressive." Expressive communicators vigorously defend their right to "just be honest," often with destructive consequences. They draw upon legitimate cultural values like the importance of honesty and openness but take these commitments to the extreme, oversimplifying the nature of effective communication in the process. All communication accomplishes multiple goals; honest expression can be one, but some important others include tact, respect, empathy, and investment in an ongoing relationship. While honest communication is laudable in the context of multiple communicative goals, taken by itself it can be used like a club to verbally punish others, with all the finesse of the proverbial bull in a china shop.

A much better alternative to either automatic or expressive communication is conscious or strategic communication. With this approach, leaders pause to consider the goals of their message, the likely response of their audience, the appropriate timing of their delivery, and the best medium for their message. As we increase our awareness of the stimulus-response patterns in our lives, we can also explore a wider range of options for how to respond. We can see the seemingly automatic stimulus-response habits that can compromise our effectiveness as leaders, teachers, parents, and colleagues.

When we purposefully *pause* between the stimulus and response, we take time to quickly assess not just what we want to say, but more importantly *what we hope to accomplish by saying it.* This important pause can be the same amount of time that it takes to inhale and exhale one breath. It is incredibly helpful to take a moment to consider what you want to accomplish and to choose words that will help you to succeed. Specifically, we should consider our intent, or the desired result of what we hope to see after our message is received and understood. Our desired results should inform the content, method of delivery, and potential follow-up needed to achieve this intent. In truth, we have this opportunity every time we speak, not just with work-related formal discussions, but also with family-related informal conversations. Unfortunately, many people only think about *what* they want to say without taking the next step of envisioning what they want to accomplish.

> **When we purposefully pause between the stimulus and response, we take time to quickly assess not just what we want to say, but more importantly what we hope to accomplish by saying it.**

Some professions have made progress in educating practitioners on how to become more conscious of the relationship between talk and action. When a surgeon asks for a specific instrument, the fulfillment of that request is having that specific instrument appear in his/her hand positioned perfectly for the surgeon's next action with it. When the fire department dispatcher communicates with firefighters, the fulfillment of these communications is providing the needed services to the right location as quickly as possible. It would be ridiculous to consider these communications effective or successful if the incorrect surgical instrument was given, or if the fire trucks arrived at the wrong house! In many professions, effective communication has a tangible, observable outcome.

That said, many more of us work in environments where the consequences of our communication are less tangible or observable. This can lead us to develop beliefs about how we are communicating which are not true. In these environments, we are taught to give opinions, to express ourselves, to give talks, to write about things that interest us, to send messages, to look and sound good during interviews, and perhaps even to publish our ideas. In most communication, the bar for success is the *expression* of the points to one or more receivers, not whether the receivers actually understood and can act on what was said. Supervisors tell their employees what to do. If the work is not done, then the problem is believed to reside with the employee. There is a presumption that if the supervisor said it, then the message was (automatically) received and understood. This is tantamount to throwing a ball into the air, in any direction, and believing that the right person will always catch it at the right time! Furthermore, this way of thinking sets up the receiver as the irresponsible party for not catching it, even if the ball were thrown in the opposite direction.

When we take the operating room staff out of the surgical theater, or the firefighters out of their fire station, those very same people also tend to slip into unconsciousness about this communication principle. Each day is filled with conversations about sports, television shows, food, cars, and work with no concrete purpose or intended outcome for such conversations except to share opinions and/or to kill time. Talking can feel good. Taking turns talking helps both people feel good. If someone does not feel he or she has had a fair amount of talk time, then the other party can be accused of monopolizing the conversation, even if that conversation is simply taking turns offering monologues. For the most part, those who are engaged in these interactions want to share something, to tell somebody something, to let people know about something. People throw thousands of words around every day with little expectation of accomplishing anything tangible other than expressing what is on their mind.

Of course, at times something tangible is indeed intended to happen. Someone may need to get picked up for a ride to work, someone may need to buy some groceries in order to prepare a meal, or someone may need to get a car repaired. Unfortunately, the talk when physical outcomes are needed sounds much the same as when no physical outcomes are required.

Leaders can rarely afford the luxury of casual, mindless communication—of unfocused self-expression—without also considering the higher responsibility of anticipating how they will be perceived, and the likelihood that their comments will have the intended practical result. This public accountability for one's communication is one of the things that makes leadership so challenging. If we become better aware of our purposes in communicating, we are then challenged to find the best words to communicate our purposes to others in a way that enables them to grasp the message as we intend, which in turn makes the desired action more likely. The next chapter explores how to do this in a way that is most effective.

CHAPTER FIVE

Checking for Grasping

I n the world of objects, all giving and taking is physical. When someone gives an object to someone else, success is recognized when the receiver is in possession of the object. We routinely pass papers, files, pens, and cups of coffee to each other. Even when mailing objects, success is defined as when the mailed object comes into the possession of the intended receiver. This is as true around the dinner table when asking for someone to pass the salt as it is core to the businesses of FedEx and UPS. Simply stated, the "giving" of an object is *not* complete *until the object is received.*

The same is true for throwing things. When preparing to throw a ball, a person will look at the intended receiver, assess the person's ability to catch it, survey the space between them, calculate the amount of force necessary to propel the ball far enough to reach the receiver. The thrower also considers any challenges (wind, trees, etc.) taking them into account, and then throws the ball, continuing to watch the ball until seeing the receiver's successful (or unsuccessful) catch. The key here is that to ensure the other person can catch what is thrown, the thrower must take other factors into account in preparing for and making the throw (i.e., do I have their attention, are they tall or short, do I throw it fast and straight or slow with an arc, are they right- or left-handed?) with the intended result of thrower being a successful catch.

Now think for a moment about how differently people behave when they prepare to "send" a message. Physically, most people understand that the intended outcome of giving or throwing something is that the other person can grasp it. In communication, however, many people do not focus so much on the receiver as they do to their intention and expression of the idea, the articulation of the argument, or the personal importance of the subject. However, just as in throwing a ball, communication has not happened until the receiver gets it—until they *grasp* the intended message. All too often communicators are so focused on the design of their own communication, ensuring that the wording is elegant and impressive, that they forget to check for grasping. Sadly, we have also known some leaders who simply do not care if their receivers grasp the message. Some have even verbalized they expect their direct reports to read their minds or figure it out.

To carry this metaphor to its logical completion, this would be the same as a person throwing a ball by:

- *ignoring* the intended receiver,

- *ignoring* the person's ability to catch it,

- *ignoring* the space between them,

- *ignoring* the amount of force necessary to propel the ball far enough to reach the receiver,

- *ignoring* any conditions (wind, trees, etc.) which should be taken into account,

- throwing the ball, with the elegance and grace of a *Sports Illustrated* cover pose,

- *ignoring* the ball after it left their fingers, and finally

- *ignoring* the receiver's successful (or unsuccessful) catch.

Clearly, such a throw would not be caught, except by random luck or an incredibly skilled receiver. However, this is what happens all the time with unconscious communication. To make matters worse, when such a message is not received successfully (i.e., when the ball is not caught), the sender invariably blames the receiver.

A director of a seven-person team in a manufacturing plant contacted me because he felt that his team was not as productive as they should be. His assessment was that they did not listen well enough to his instructions. His goal when he delegated tasks was to express himself clearly, and to his own satisfaction. His criteria for effective delegation were that he first outlined his directive in advance, and then described what was needed, consistent with his outline. He was so interested in communicating clearly and accurately that he would typically ask his staff *not* to interrupt him while he was giving assignments because he did not want to lose his place (!). After he was done with the description of the assignments, he then opened the floor for questions. There never were any. The lack of questions further convinced him that he was an excellent communicator. When the work failed to get done, his only reasonable conclusion was that his staff had not listened properly—after all, he *knew* he was a good communicator.

He originally contacted me to train his staff how to listen better—to improve their listening skills, which appeared to him to be a perfectly reasonable diagnosis of the problem given his assumptions about his own excellent communication skills. He also believed he was a good communicator with his children, his wife, and everyone else he encountered. He was unaware of the fundamental principle that it is the *receiver* who defines meaning, not the speaker (see chapter one).

Although we all pass physical things to each other throughout the day, we are mostly unconscious of the complex assessment process that we use each time. Yet by and large, we do this flawlessly. At the same time, most are also unaware that this same "assessment of grasping" can be applied when giving assignments (or opinions, information, or advice). This means that it is actually possible (and highly desirable) to assess if people we speak with have grasped the meaning as we intended.

When one person hands another person a hot cup of coffee, the individuals in fact *work together* to ensure the coffee is not spilled. The person giving the coffee conducts a sophisticated (but mostly unconscious) analysis of the gradual transition of moving the cup from the giver's hand to the receiver's hand. The giver of the coffee watches the receiver, feels the weight of the cup, and watches the control being transferred from his own hand to the receiver's hand. If the receiver is elderly, young, short, tall, sick, or healthy, then the giver modifies the assessment accordingly, yet *never, ever lets go* of the cup until they feel that the receiver has a firm grasp on it. The giver's criteria for success is the cup of coffee in the receiver's hands with nothing spilled and with no one's hands burned from the hot coffee. The speaker's criteria for success can be knowing the message was grasped as intended.

Speaking with purpose and assessing for grasping involves the following three steps:

1. Clearly define the ultimate desired outcome

2. Choose language that is meaningful to your receiver

3. Monitor grasping during the conversation and assess if it has ocurred before deciding if you have successfully communicated

STEP 1: CLEARLY DEFINE THE ULTIMATE DESIRED OUTCOME.

All too often, we know what we want to say and see happen; however, we tend to confuse this ultimate performance outcome with our own outputs—activities that may contribute to the outcome but are not in and of themselves the ultimate desired goal. For example, if you are trying to improve customer satisfaction, your desired outcome may be identified as evidence of improved scores on a customer survey. Some years ago, the American Cancer Society measured the effectiveness of their own communication efforts by the number of posters they had distributed (they no longer use this measure). The point is that leaders all too often become preoccupied with the messages they send to promote these changes—with the booklets, websites, retreats, training programs, and meetings, all intended to engage employees. While these methods may all be important, it is critical to focus on the true desired outcome as a way of staying connected to what is tangibly happening as a result of your efforts. It is critically important to not confuse communication attempts—the various methods you may have tried to get your message across—and actual communication, how the message was in fact received, and what was ultimately done with the message.

STEP 2: CHOOSE LANGUAGE THAT IS MEANINGFUL TO YOUR RECEIVER.

It is much more likely that receivers will grasp your meaning if you speak in a language that they find familiar. For example, middle managers will be more effective if they translate top management messages for their employees in a way that makes the messages relevant to their employees' work. Similarly, middle managers should encourage their next level down supervisors to do the same thing as they tailor the message to their respective employees. This is in contrast to the common cascade message rollout, where the same exact words get repeated to every individual in the organization, with varying levels of interpretation and uneven success.

I have seen this principle extended to include the vocabulary that is used by clients and customers. I was asked to facilitate a potentially contentious board meeting for a local charity that supported new refugees to the US. In my conversations with board members, I realized that they had completely lost sight of their mission—their ultimate desired outcome—and as a result, they had become conflicted over matters of technical policy and insider politics. Consequently, I chose to open the board meeting with live testimony from five refugees that the organization had recently helped, asking them to tell their stories in their own words and to describe what the organization's work had meant to them. After their stories, the board meeting proceeded in a much more amicable and productive fashion. The leaders had been reminded of their true desired outcome—refugee support—in language that was all but impossible to ignore. In all communication, the focus on the desired outcome needs to remain more important than the process or mechanism used to send the message.

STEP 3: MONITOR GRASPING DURING THE CONVERSATION AND ASSESS IF IT HAS OCURRED BEFORE DECIDING IF YOU HAVE SUCCESSFULLY COMMUNICATED.

Evidence of grasping can occur spontaneously. While giving assignments, effective leaders will observe their audience closely for any sign of confusion or hesitation. Some people may interrupt to ask questions, which can be evidence of an attempt to grasp what is being communicated. Some people may appear puzzled, in which case the speaker can pause and wait for people in the audience to respond with questions or reactions. Some people may paraphrase the assignment in their own words or offer that these instructions appear similar to something that was done previously. All these responses may serve as evidence that members of the audience are understanding the assignment and the tangible outcome that is desired. Even if someone offers criticism of the ideas being presented, it can provide good evidence that they are grasping the message. When someone responds with criticism there is an opportunity to ask that person to continue to share their criticism in the service of a deeper understanding.

Most spontaneous disagreements are with the receiver's inaccurate perception of what is being expressed by the speaker. Encouraging people to give more details about their disagreements usually enables them to become more conscious of the speaker's intent. In this way people can eventually talk themselves into the desired understanding. This is much better than the more common practice: the speaker shutting down questions and simply repeating the instructions over and over again, comfortable in the illusion that greater clarity is achieved by the audience when, in fact, only the speaker is feeling that they have been clearer after each repetition! By exploring potential disagreements and misunderstandings, the audience's responses enable the speaker to know that the meaning of the message is understood, and which aspects may be problematic. Often such responses can give the speaker greater confidence that the ultimate desired tangible outcome will be achieved, the meaning will be received, the ideas will be grasped, and appropriate actions will follow.

In our professional lives, we have had the opportunity to observe thousands of bright, accomplished individuals speak to large groups. In a small but significant percentage of these events, something happens that creates a distraction or disconnect between the speaker and the audience—it can be the room temperature(too hot or cold), distracting noises coming from outside, or problems with technology. Direct sunlight on the screen where slides are being shown can make it impossible for the audience to read the slides. When the overhead PA system cuts out half or more of the participants can no longer hear the speaker. What amazes us in these instances are the number of smart, accomplished people who will "press on" with what they have to say, despite the fact that their audience is obviously disengaged or distracted. This desire by many to "just get through it" reveals once again the fundamental mistake people make when they equate "delivering" their message with having successfully communicated something.

Not everyone is this impervious, thankfully. Many communicators make some attempt to determine whether their message is getting through as intended. Toward this end, they may ask questions to ascertain whether or not grasping has occurred. Unfortunately, if the speaker asks a question that receives a "yes" or "sure" response, then there is still no evidence of grasping. Functionally, the words "yes" and "sure" work as polite turn taking cues, not as any kind of evidence of grasping. As such, the following "yes/no" questions *never, ever, ever work*:

- "Does everyone understand?"
- "Do you think you can get this done?"
- "Can we make this deadline?"
- "Can you finish phase one by next Friday?"
- "Isn't this a worthwhile project?"
- "Do you have what you need to get this done?"
- "Isn't this going to be a fun project?"

We do not mean to suggest that people lie when they routinely nod affirmatively in response to each of these general queries. Rather, most people are deeply committed to saving face, both their own and their boss's. As such, most people will invariably politely agree with these questions. The main reason a "yes" response cannot be considered evidence of grasping is that by saying "yes," the respondent is actually communicating the following: "Yes, I believe I know the assignment, and I believe I know what is expected, and I believe I can read your mind, and that my gut will guide me to get this work done the way that I think I understand you want it done." This, however, is definitely not evidence of grasping.

Imagine a musician in a band believing that her purpose was to play some notes, notes that she enjoys playing. These notes may have nothing to do with what the rest of the band is doing. To the extent that the musician's goal is personal expression, she will have a difficult time finding others to join her band. Four musicians expressing themselves without regard to each other's interests and needs makes for a very poor band. If a musician's goal is to be a soloist, the problem remains. Someone playing notes that are self-pleasing, independent of playing a violin or flute in accord with a specific musical piece, could be a soloist, though perhaps only at home. To be a successful soloist, the performer needs to express herself in a way that enables a conductor to know where she is, a page turner to know when to turn the page, a string section to know when to pick up the piece. Good musicians do more than express themselves; they deliberately connect with and enable others to grasp their roles, responses, and turns. Within their connection, there is also room for personal expression. But expression alone is insufficient for success.

José loves singing in the shower. He is proud of all the sounds he can make to emphasize different parts of the songs he singes.

His self-expression is beautiful—to him. One night, José visited a karaoke bar filled with people who, he thought, would enjoy his performance. Nearly half the people left the bar during his performance. José apparently thought, as so many leaders do, that self-expression, with confidence, was all that was needed to be effective with others. This is a decision nearly all unconscious communicators make. The temptation to believe that if I just tell people the thoughts in my head, and if I speak slowly enough and if I even read these thoughts off of a PowerPoint slide, they will have to get it. If they do not, then there must be something wrong with them. This faulty logic enables unconscious leaders to perpetuate their unconsciousness—without conscious analysis of our own contribution to enabling other to grasp our music/wisdom, we can persist in just blaming the audience, or our employees.

A conscious communicator has a purpose that touches the receiver in some way and accomplishes something. The goal of giving a compliment becomes the goal of saying something that contributes to the other person feeling proud about what he/she has done. The goal of giving feedback becomes having a conversation with someone that enables that person to describe what he or she can do differently the next time to achieve a better outcome. The goal of thanking someone becomes the goal of saying some things that result in that person feeling appreciated and recognized. Effective communication does not end with the speaker making sounds; it ends with something being accomplished.

When the cashier at the window of a fast food restaurant has the goal of *giving* you your change, far more money gets blown away during this transaction than when the customer has the goal of *making certain the cashier receives* the money. The customer, consciously or unconsciously, has a material interest in passing money in such a way that guarantees the cashier can receive it. If the money is dropped, no food. The cashier, on the other hand, has little to no material interest in the transaction. The money is not his, the food is not his, and any consequences about dropping the money while giving change has little to no effect on him. If a dollar of change blows away, the customer is the person who has to get out of the car and chase the money. The goal of giving something is fundamentally different from the goal of ensuring someone gets something.

This also applies to aspects of our physical life—if my goal is to throw you a Frisbee, I may throw it at you and hope that you are skilled enough to catch it. If you offered me five dollars to throw the Frisbee in a way that guarantees the receiver is able to *catch* it, I, and most people in general, would throw the Frisbee differently—more consciously. The goal/outcome influences both our physical and verbal behavior.

When the discharge nurse at a children's hospital meets with the parents, if the nurse's goal is to "give them the discharge instructions" he/she may read them quickly and close with "Any questions?" spoken so quickly a normal person, let alone a stressed parent, has no time to think. And then the parents and sick child are ushered out. When the discharge nurse's goal is for the discharge instructions to be *understood and followed*, a conscious communicator will give a copy of the instructions to the parents and, while reviewing them (as opposed to reading them), ask the parents questions about some of the instructions, such as, "Your son will need a lot of medication. What kind of a system have you thought about for keeping track of these medications?" or "Your daughter will not be able to go swimming because of her cast. How do you think she will handle this during these hot summer months?" The discharge nurse could also engage the child with questions like, "What will you be able to do to keep your cast clean?"

If the purpose of talking is to express oneself, then we propose that there is no material purpose or intended outcome beyond expression. Expressing oneself is not communicating effectively. Alternatively, if the purpose of talking is to persuade someone to take care of a cast, or to take medications the right way, or to improve performance, then the receiver must be engaged, and the speaker must carefully observe the receiver to assess that the message being sent during the conversation is being understood by the receiver in order to assess success.

In summary, we have all accumulated beliefs about communication that may or may not be helpful to us or others. We have a choice. We can become more conscious and aware of our communication practices and assumptions and learn how to become more effective as communicators; or we can cling to our myths and blame everybody else for having poor communication and needing listening training.

Earlier we promised to provide a more detailed review of constructive questions that have proven to have value when caring about and actively checking for grasping. These questions have greatest value when evidence of grasping has not spontaneously occurred. For much of our personal and work lives, evidence of grasping may not be so obvious. When I ask an employee to move up a deadline by two weeks and he replies, "OK," I likely have no clue that he understands what is needed, who else needs to be contacted, or the impact on resources or cost. Questions that solicit a "yes" or "no" answer typically are just polite turn-taking questions. Polite people, meaning no harm, will typically reply "yes" or "sure" to such questions.

To better assess grasping, consider the following examples of better questions.

WEAK QUESTION	BETTER QUESTION	IMPLICATION
Can you get this done two weeks sooner?	In order to move up the deadline on this project by two weeks, what do you think some of the implications will be regarding staffing, supplies, and cost to make this move?	The response to this question is much more likely to provide evidence that the employee has or has not grasped the need and the implications of the deadline shift.
Does everyone understand the new procedure?	What are some of the challenges we might encounter with this new procedure, and how do you think our customers might respond to these new protocols?	With this question, your audience is respectfully invited to contribute to their own detailed understanding of the new procedure.
Do you think we can make this deadline?	What specific details do we need to pay close attention to in order to ensure that we will make this deadline?	This question will help you feel comfortable that your team can focus on requirements to make the deadline or will help you realize your team is not going to be successful, and will need actions besides proceeding with blind faith.
Can you get me a draft of your report by next Friday?	So that I can review a draft of your report by next Friday, what is the earliest date and time you can get it to me?	Asking someone to commit to a self-identified specific date and time is realistic and much more powerful than making up a deadline and asking for a yes/no reply.
Do you have what you need to get this done?	What are the top four or five things you will need in order to get this done?	If the reply includes needs appropriate to this task, then the leader can feel more secure that grasping has occurred than if the employee had just said, sure.

Some additional generic "grasping" questions include the following:

1. How long do you think it will take?

2. Who will you need to involve in order to maximize your success?

3. How do you plan to subdivide this complex assignment into phases or sections?

4. What would help you ensure your success with this assignment?

5. Given all your priorities, what other projects might need to be delayed or delegated in order for you to meet the new deadline?

6. Among all your priorities, where would you rank this project/task?

7. Who do you think could help you with this?

8. Who do you think will benefit from this?

9. Are there other individuals or departments who might be interested in this project and how would you approach them about it?

10. How would you know you were successful?

11. What are your first steps going to be?

12. As you scope out this project, what do you think you will include in your first update to me and when can I expect it?

13. Which of your talents do you think will be most helpful in getting this done?

Here is further testimony from a leader who shared with us an epiphany that he had about the power of asking the right kinds of follow-up questions:

I was at a conference and during one of the breaks, I told one of my employees that I had a six-month project for her to take on. I described the three phases of the project at great length and told her how important this work was for our department and for our organization. She nodded in seeming agreement as I described the project. When I was done talking, I felt that I had been quite clear and detailed in my explanation. I asked her if she thought she could get it done, and she said, "Yes." I asked her if she had all the resources she needed to get it done, and she said, "Yes."

But then I remembered that you had told me that "yes" is not evidence of grasping. I thought about a question that would require her to reflect a deeper understanding of what I had just explained. I asked one more question that told me everything I wanted to know: "How long do you think each of the three phases of this project will take?" Her response was, "What were the names of the phases?"

I then apologized as I realized I was speaking at her, not with her. I had thrown my idea at her and given her no space to ask questions and engage. I had thrown my ideas [remembering the ball metaphor] at her so hard she could not possibly have caught them. If I did not check for grasping, then I would have deluded myself into thinking that my instructions were clear, and then blamed her for not listening when it was time to deliver on the project.

The leader's follow-up question in this case was excellent. Yes-or-no questions ask employees to only be respectful. Asking a question that requires an understanding and application of the ideas presented is the best way to ascertain if grasping has occurred. Such probing questions by the leader are needed if evidence of grasping is not demonstrated during the delegation by useful questions from the employee. There are many reasons an employee does not interrupt a boss to ask questions. Most of these reasons involve saving face, not wanting to look stupid, not wanting to appear disrespectful, not wanting to reveal personal confusion for fear it would be attributed to the employee's low IQ rather than the leader's inarticulate and excited babble.

If she had asked questions during the delegation, or had been invited to ask questions, it would have helped her grasp the assignment and provided confidence to her boss that grasping had occurred. In the absence of any spontaneous evidence of grasping, the leader (the person who has the goal) needed to ask a question that would provide evidence of grasping—or evidence of no grasping. Finding out that someone does not know what he/she is supposed to do is also critical, and the earlier such a misunderstanding is revealed the greater are the overall chances for success.

CHAPTER SIX

Grasping, Quality, and Safety

E arly humans coped with a hostile environment by organizing to do things collectively that would be impossible as individuals. Up until the Industrial Revolution, most of this organizing occurred in families, tribes, and small communities. The lone exception was the formation of large armies, which were rigidly organized by specialization and hierarchical level.

Since industrialization, the military model came to be applied across most types of organizations and industries, from factories to prisons to schools. While specialization and division of labor makes sense as one way of dealing with complexity, it creates another serious problem. As people come to function in separate disciplinary silos, their ability to collaborate with others in different specializations decreases significantly including their ability to see the big picture. Engineers don't talk to salespeople; emergency room doctors live in a different world from pharmacists and social workers. In academia, a commonly heard criticism is that that while communities have problems, universities have disciplines. Overspecialization into silos eventually erodes the organization's ability to function effectively on behalf of its customers and stakeholders.

Customers, on the other hand, have no interest in the effectiveness of individual silos—they only care about the quality of the final product or service, which is dependent upon successful horizontal collaboration across what some have called the "white spaces in the organizational chart." Nothing is more frustrating to a customer than being told by someone in one part of an organization that there is nothing they can do to solve a problem generated somewhere else in the same organization! This frustration has led to the creation of multiple bridging mechanisms, such as one-stop shops and case-management systems, all designed to encourage constructive connections within the organization in the service of creating a better experience for the customer.

But what does any of this have to do with grasping? Quite a bit, in fact. The horizontal processes that customers experience as they move through the organization are made up of countless "handoffs" across specialized silos. In American manufacturing, for decades engineers wanted to have little to do with nonengineers and consequently would design products that were difficult to build and contained features that few people wanted to buy. In the realm of mental health care, patients might be screened and diagnosed effectively but have difficulty finding the proper health professionals to address their diagnoses. The list goes on and on. And all of these difficulties occur because people in different silos speak different languages, have differing priorities, and are often not skilled in "handing off" information to others outside of their area in a way that works for patients or customers. Interdepartmental communication in all organizations is challenging and one reason is that individuals do not do a good job of checking for grasping when they communicate across silos.

In a real sense, the competitiveness of manufacturing in the US was saved by a renewed focus on collaboration and grasping. Some of you may be familiar with Total Quality Management (TQM), a movement that first took root in Japan and swept across the US in the late twentieth century. One of the tenets of TQM was that improving manufacturing processes required people from different silos to work together to map the current process flow and identify critical handoffs where their departments served as "internal" customers and suppliers. Once identified, the goal was to ensure that the two sides understood each other so well that internal suppliers could agree to "only pass on quality" as defined by the internal customer! Quality metrics were defined based upon the requirements of the receiver, not the preferences, judgment, or expertise of the sender. This created a seismic shift in how formerly siloed employees worked together, the result being dramatic improvements in the ultimate quality of products.

Schools and universities are also undergoing a sea change in how they work to ensure the success of their students. Historically, universities would admit qualified students and hope for the best. Each part of the university worked hard to execute its specialized function. Admissions admitted a talented class, faculty taught the material, and residence hall managers tried to provide a positive campus living experience. But while this uncoordinated approach worked out for many students, a large minority fell through the white spaces in the organizational chart; and when they failed, the failure almost always had something to do with a lack of communication and collaboration. People in silo A recognized that a student was struggling but never alerted silo B. People in finance accepted payment for a student to retake a course for the tenth time without taking responsibility for what was happening to that student. Today, nearly every school is working to create alignment among departments to serve students, which requires regular communication across departments. To make this work, people must learn about the language, values and priorities of others so they can understand how to best engage with them in a way that will actually be successful.

The ability to assess grasping is an essential process to reduce health-care handoff errors. Medical errors conservatively contribute to between sixty thousand and one hundred thousand deaths a year. Communication errors are a large part of medical error. A small hospital in central Massachusetts requested our assistance with improving handoffs a few years ago.. Their specific focus was twofold: shift handoffs and patient discharges. In both cases, very caring and highly capable health-care professionals invested considerable time preparing reports that would go to the next shift or to the parents of the discharged children. Too often people on the receiving shifts and parents did not take the time to read the materials they were given.

One of the first things we did was to assess the documents they were using during these handoffs. We found fifth-generation faded photocopies of forms with insufficient space for staff to write anything that could be read easily by the receivers of these documents. One of the first steps we took was to redesign their forms so that they could be completed either on the computer or by hand—with ample space for writing down the key information.

We were also concerned that these communications were largely one way. The information was intended to be delivered, sent, and communicated to someone else (thrown—remember the ball metaphor). Shift reports were prepared for nurses and physicians, and extensive documentation packets were prepared for parents. We decided to provide a workshop that would enable them to become conscious about the goal of pursuing grasping as central to effective communication, not just throwing words. The one-hour workshop was designed to enable them to literally feel objects being grasped. We used several objects such as paper clips, rubber bands, pens, and papers. We then transitioned the workshop to demonstrate that the same kind of confidence of grasping was achievable with oral communication. We followed the workshop with a forty-five-minute laboratory during which the participants developed their own appropriate grasping questions for a variety of real-work situations. The following are some real-life examples.

Shift change:

> While reviewing the report on a specific patient, doing so in the patient's room so that he or she can ask questions is very helpful. Under these circumstances, incoming staff are much more likely to ask questions of the outgoing staff because they want to assure the patient of the continuity of care. If the receiving shift nurse has no questions (constituting no evidence of grasping) the outgoing nurse could ask, "How often will you be looking in on Joey?" or "Who else is on the schedule to be looking in on Joey?" or "Joey had an operation this morning and can have lots of Jell-O tonight. Who should be his Jell-O provider tonight?" Any question that gets a person talking is better than either no questions or yes/no questions.

Patient discharge:

> Discharging patients in a children's hospital has dramatic implications. The patient him or herself has little understanding of the complications of his/her care. Parents and guardians are stressed and worried about their ability to meet their child's needs at home. When discharging patients

under these circumstances some hospitals put a great deal of effort into getting extensive written details to the parents/guardians. They quite reasonably do not want to leave anything out. Unfortunately, the quality and quantity of information provided to someone has little relationship to whether or not the most critical information has been grasped. *By paying attention to the volume of information being given to the parent, the discharge staff can miss opportunities to assure grasping.* Too often discharge staff throw words at families and then follow up with "So do you think you will be able to take care of your child?" What parent in his or her right mind would say, "I am not sure at all. I am frightened, I have to go to work, and I am not sure if my babysitter (or mother or grandmother) will be as responsible as I think I am. What do I do if my child gets worse? I cannot afford all the medications, so I plan on cutting all the pills in half." Grasping the instructions to effectively care for a child after a hospital stay is far more important than leaving with a pile of paper that may go unread.

The individual managing the discharge knows more about the patient's needs at the time of discharge than the parent or guardian. This person can summarize what is needed, and if several questions arise, he/she can feel confident grasping is occurring. If there are no questions, it is useful to ask questions about the parent/guardian's understanding of some (not all) of the more complex instructions, such as these:

- Your child has many medications she needs several times a day. I would have trouble keeping track of all of them. What kind of system will you use?

- I have reviewed many instructions with you. What part of this do you think might be the hardest for you to do?

- We have learned that many parents worry about bothering us on weekends, and that frankly scares me. I do not want you to worry about us. We are here to help your child. To help me feel more comfortable, what kinds of symptoms could show up that you would call us about?

Effective communicators must be conscious of their desired outcome—which is the receiver's grasping. The creative time for formulating purpose is in the space (pause) between the stimulus and the response. We assess grasping of every item we physically give to anyone. The process we use to do this is largely unconscious. We can become more conscious of this assessment and apply the process to oral communication. Rather than just give advice, give a compliment, or react, we can engage people we work with in ways that enable us to assess whether or not they grasp what we intend. Their responses are essentially feedback that we can use to calibrate if more dialogue is necessary or if they "got it." Too often, when people have a sick feeling in their stomachs that they are not being understood they resort to repeating themselves or speaking louder. Neither of these strategies increase the likelihood of grasping. The best solution is to ask one or two good questions. The other person's responses, essentially feedback, will let us know if grasping is occurring or if more work is needed. As with physical grasping, we should not walk away or "let go" until we have confidence grasping has occurred.

There is another subtle point to be made about questions. Note that the pursuit of questions is intended to both gain evidence of grasping *and* also to show respect. Good questions intended to assess grasping originate in concern for others and for the total organization.

Good questions flow from our humility, perhaps we may not have been clear, or we may not have been as thorough as we would have hoped. Good questions also flow from the belief that the people we are speaking with are trying to understand what we mean. No one deliberately chooses not to listen during a conversation. Unfortunately, unconscious communicators are easily distracted, both as speakers and listeners. Therefore, we need to develop better questions to be sure that our receiver is engaged. Statements like the following are unacceptable because they offer no assurance of comprehension.

The pursuit of questions is intended to both gain evidence of grasping and also to show respect.

Never say any of the following:

- I have tried to explain this project to you, and I do not trust you know how to listen (as opposed to the truth, which would be I do not trust my own ability to explain instructions), so please repeat back what I said.

- I need to be sure that you understand, so tell me exactly what I said.

- I am done explaining, so repeat it all back to me now.

- You do not look like you understand, so I am going to repeat myself several times.

- This is a very important assignment. You had better give it all you've got, OK?

Indeed, strategic communicators are conscious communicators. They consider their goals and audiences—and potential unanticipated consequences—before they speak or write. Conscious communication, especially for beginners, can be exhausting. Some people, therefore, may use expressive communication with friends when out to dinner or at a concert. Nevertheless, working leaders see communication as a tool to be used carefully, and they see their communicative acts as much more than automatic or spontaneous expressions of thoughts or feelings. They see communication acts as strategic choices with consequences. They know that their leadership effectiveness is dependent upon being conscious communicators, and they work at moving in the direction of heightened awareness each day.

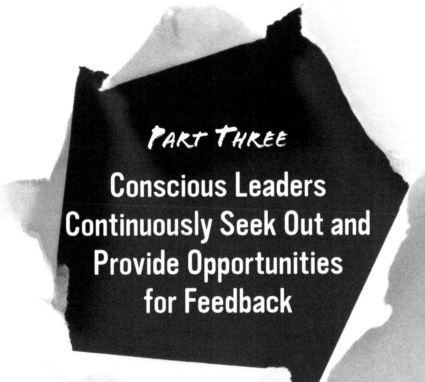

PART THREE

Conscious Leaders
Continuously Seek Out and
Provide Opportunities
for Feedback

Chapter Seven

Feedback Is Everywhere

he concept of feedback is one of the most misunderstood within communication. Over time, the notion that feedback about one's talk and actions is both abundant and readily available has been replaced by a much narrower definition that is limited to specific, purposeful acts initiated by a supervisor. At a recent communication workshop we conducted, we began by asking the participating leaders for some examples of feedback. Every single person in the room offered examples similar to the following:

- Feedback is when I *tell* an employee that she is doing good work.

- Feedback is when I *give* my employees their performance reviews.

- Feedback is when I *let my employees know* that they are doing a good job.

- Feedback is when I *tell* an employee he needs to do better work.

Each leader in attendance described feedback as a message the leader created and relayed to the employee. Feedback was consistently described as something that leaders have the responsibility to *supply* to employees, something they dispense with the aim of either rewarding or correcting behavior. The underlying assumption here is both pervasive and wrong—that employees will not know if they are doing good or bad work *unless their leader tells them so.*

We suspect that one of the reasons this narrow definition of feedback has emerged is that there are an abundance of HR trainers and consultants who focus on teaching leaders how to coach their employees—and in particular those employees who are not performing well. This work is important given the nature of the employment relationship in modern capitalist societies, where it can be difficult to remove or replace a poor performer without clear evidence of "progressive discipline" and a "performance improvement plan" indicating that serious attempts were made to help the employee to succeed. While this is in one sense understandable, it distracts us from the true, *organic* nature of feedback as it occurs naturally in every work environment.

When employees and leaders become conscious of how feedback occurs naturally in the world, both can become more empowered, and can collaborate and improve together in a highly accountable work environment. Setting aside for a moment the narrow idea of feedback as something that a supervisor "gives" an employee, consider the following familiar examples of naturally occurring, real-life examples of feedback:

- Taking a hot bowl out of the oven without an oven mitt and burning your hand

- Driving a car on the highway and drifting onto the rumble strip—feeling the vibration and hearing the noise

- Experiencing "brain freeze" while drinking an ice cream milkshake too quickly

- Getting a gutter ball when bowling

- Drinking milk that has turned sour and spitting it out

- Seeing a pot of boiling pasta, potatoes, spinach, etc., boil over onto the stove top

- Glancing at a car's speedometer

- Opening mail and getting a paper cut

- Using a meat thermometer to assess if certain foods are adequately cooked

- Running out of propane on the barbecue

- Taking a photograph and then noticing the picture is blurry or out of focus

- Hitting one's thumb when driving a nail

- Shooting foul shots at a basket and making or failing to make them

- Taking golf swings at a driving range

The bottom line is this: *Feedback is everywhere if we know where to look for it.* Learning to recognize naturally occurring feedback—and to take responsibility for using it to improve our performance—should be our goal. Unfortunately, there are

The bottom line is this: Feedback is everywhere if we know where to look for it.

two reasons why people may ignore naturally occurring sources of useful information. The first is that it doesn't immediately feel good to acknowledge subpar performance. Imagine taking a practice test (like the SAT or GMAT) and getting a low score. While many people would use this feedback to improve their study strategy, others will conclude that there is "something wrong with the test." Using the examples above, imagine someone finding fault with the height of the basketball hoop, the lens in their camera, or their golf club. If the negative feelings associated with constructive feedback are too much, people often blame other people and things for their performance challenges.

The second reason why people ignore naturally occurring feedback is that we have trained them to do so—to keep their head down and work, and to wait to receive feedback from an "authorized" source such as a supervisor. This trained incapacity to learn and make improvements on one's own can be comical and even tragic. A number of years ago I noticed that the plants that were placed on the sunny side of my university library routinely died. When I approached the gardener doing the planting, he told me that these plants didn't do well in direct sunlight, which was typical for this side of the building. When I asked why he continued to replace them despite this obvious problem, he explained that his supervisor insisted on it.

Becoming conscious of feedback is inextricably linked to becoming conscious of our personal responsibilities in the world. The more responsible we are in all that we do, the more we look to find how our behavior has contributed to the results we see in the world. The less responsible we are, the more we live in a world that all seemingly negative experiences are other people's fault, and in which we wait for others to tell us how we are doing.

Leaders who have employees who rate their engagement as low, or who receive low scores on customer satisfaction assessments are free to irresponsibly moan that today's employees have lost their work ethic, are too old or too young to care, need more training, need stronger performance evaluations at the end of the year, need more account-ability or are lazy. Such leaders might also erroneously conclude their employees need more feedback and then schedule more one-on-one meetings to more clearly tell them everything they are doing wrong.

Conscious leaders behave differently and ask, "How might I be contributing to my employees' performance, productivity, customer/patient service, and experience?" If, at the beginning of a conversation, you are happy and excited, but then at the end of the encounter you are frustrated or angry—I am the variable. Something I said or did has contributed to this outcome. Your responses to me are legitimate feedback about how I conducted myself—if I want to lead responsibly.

For a variety of reasons, not all feedback is perceived as equally useful for improving one's performance. One of the factors affecting the perceived usefulness of feedback is its timeliness. See the Timely Feedback Model in Figure 8.1 below. According to this model, the usefulness of feedback is directly proportional to the timeliness with which the performer receives it. Picking up on our earlier discussion, please note the key word here is "receive." Recall that feedback can be received directly from the environment or from others. Everything that is a response to someone's behavior can be interpreted as feedback. If I bump into someone's parked car while parking mine, hearing the noise and feeling the bump are both feedback. (Interestingly, when the owner of the other car then begins screaming at me that I just hit his car, this isn't technically feedback—I already knew that I hit his car.)

Timely Feedback Model

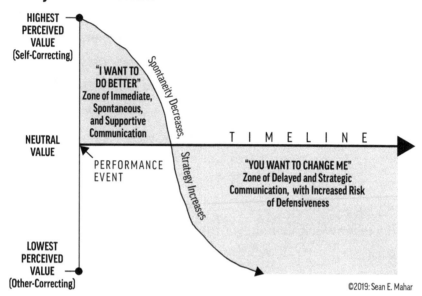

©2019: Sean E. Mahar

When I stray too far to the right while driving on the highway and encounter the rumble strip, the vibration and sound are feedback, and I self-correct. When my partner begins screaming for me to get back into the proper lane, this is not feedback; it is someone yelling.

When I make a mistake at work and, because of the mistake, have to spend a weekend reworking my spreadsheet, fixing my report, or repainting the rooms I had painted the wrong color—I have experienced the feedback needed to improve. When my boss sits down with me at the end of the week and tells me everything that I did wrong and

In the ideal world, feedback is organic, easily available, and self-correcting.

tells me the cost of my mistakes, this is not feedback, it is just someone attempting to reinforce what I already know (and demonstrate that they know it, too, and are documenting it).

In the ideal world, feedback is organic, easily available, and self-correcting. It enables responsible people to notice the effect, consequence or impact of their actions on the environment and on other people.

If I drop a fork into the garbage disposal, turn it on, and let it run for a while, the impact of all these things on the fork is feedback to me. If I am responsible, I will for many, many years look into garbage disposals before I turn them on. If I am not a responsible person, I will blame someone else for dropping the fork into the disposal, or I will blame the plumber for not installing some kind of screen over the garbage disposal, or I will blame my partner for making me wash the dishes and decide to never help out in the kitchen again.

The more time that goes by between my making a mistake and my becoming aware of that mistake, the greater the likelihood that I will be inclined to believe that anyone bringing the mistake to my attention is being hostile to me. The more time that goes by the greater will be my defensiveness. As time goes by, we tend to remember our experiences as successful, often more successful than they actually were. If you come to me a few days after I did something and try to tell me I made a mistake, most will wonder why you are making this up and attacking me. People feel defensive when they think they are being attacked.

In the Timely Feedback Model, the spontaneity curve is intended to describe the spontaneity of the supervisor, the person who may want to change the employee's behavior. When information or responses come to my attention as performer, I appreciate the opportunity to improve. If someone else wants to help me improve my performance and they can communicate such within the period of time I am receptive and seeking feedback, it still feels like feedback. If too much time goes by between my performance and someone bringing that to my attention, it will most likely be perceived as embarrassment or ill-intended criticism (or as part of the HR progressive discipline process discussed earlier—i.e., you don't want me to improve, you are building a case to fire me). The spontaneity slope is a dramatic part of the model because the more time the other person, supervisor for example, thinks about what to say and how to say it, or consults with others about the best way to bring such "constructive" criticism, the greater the likelihood that no matter what is said, I will feel attacked and defensive. True feedback is not given, mailed, emailed, or otherwise packaged. Feedback is what the performer notices in his/her environment as a response to his/her behaviors. Feedback is self-correcting. It may be painful, like when hitting my thumb with a hammer, but it is also always potentially helpful. Leaders can play a role in designing environments where this kind of immediate, unmediated feedback is available to and among employees and by supporting their use of it.

The consequences of thinking about feedback this way—as naturally occurring in the environment and available for responsible individuals to use to improve their performance—minimizes the role of other people as sources of feedback. To be sure, there are times when others' reactions and opinions are important, such as when the performance issue that needs addressing is an employee's interpersonal competency, and for which others' reactions constitute the primary data needed to make corrections. In this case, the timely feedback model is especially important, inasmuch as interpersonal feedback is especially emotionally charged, and best received quickly and in the spirit of helpful correction (as opposed to delayed and in the spirit of complaint or punishment).

That said, for most areas of performance the idea that a person can "give" feedback is akin to imagining that a canyon "gave" the yodeler an echo reply. The canyon does not independently create a message for the yodeler, it can only reflect back. Feedback is an echo back to the sender, not originated by the canyon walls. Feedback is used in echolocation by bats and porpoises, to know where they are and to navigate their environment. Bats and porpoises do not wait for cave or underwater cavern walls to shout back "here I am." They listen to the echo to get their bearings. Even when bats fly out of caves at dusk in the thousands, they do not bump into each other and shout, "Do not touch me." Each is personally responsible for his/her own navigation based on echolocation. When an airport tower uses radar to locate all the airplanes coming in for a landing, the air traffic controller does not wait for the pilot's reply, "Here I am." Rather, the air traffic controller uses radar, the signal that bounces off the airplane to verify location. When a local police officer uses the radar gun to check for motorists who are speeding, the officer does not send a message to the motorist to confirm if he or she is speeding. Rather, the radar gun is calibrated to be accurate within certain tolerances and the officer informs the driver that he or she was speeding. These are all feedback systems—a process of sending out a signal and using the echo, response, or reflected signal to confirm location and speed.

Far too many leaders still believe that if they see one of their employees make a mistake in February and June, the annual December performance review is a reasonable time to provide corrective feedback. Such logic seems unfathomable, though leaders do this all the time, all around the world. Be it arrogance or ignorance, the capacity to rationalize that I can give you feedback about something you did six months ago seems to be a function of being unconscious about how feedback works best. Since people do not know what they do not know, such leaders have no idea their practice is essentially delusional. The truth can be much simpler: If I turn the garbage disposal on with a fork in it, I own the consequences. *The true role of the leader is not to provide feedback to employees but to provide multiple mechanisms and incentives for employees to seek out naturally occurring feedback and use it to continuously improve their performance.*

The journey from being unconscious to conscious about feedback begins with becoming more physically aware of the feedback that is all around us. Musicians, mechanics, surgeons, carpenters, plumbers, technicians, nurses, painters, teachers, electricians have all mastered processing feedback in order to perform quality work. Leaders can also learn this. When first working with leaders who can benefit from increased consciousness about feedback, we often ask them to increase their awareness of the feedback all around them—when we say good morning to someone and smile and they reciprocate, that is feedback. When we compliment someone for a job well done and they say "thank you," that is feedback. When we show someone how to do something and that person, in turn, passes that skill to others, that is feedback.

When a leader interacts with someone, that person's responses are feedback. The conscious leader can learn, via practice, how to specifically look for feedback that the dialogue is productive—that the other person is grasping what is being shared and is able to appropriately act on the subject at hand. By becoming conscious of how feedback is crucial to the acquisition and development of all higher-level leadership skills and by learning how to use feedback for both our own and other's development, leaders gain a sizeable competitive advantage over those who still struggle with the illusion that only leaders have the power to give feedback. *Feedback is everywhere. Great leaders help their employees discern constructive feedback in their work environments; they do not try to control situations so that all feedback flows through them. Conscious leaders set their employees free to make improvements in everything they do.*

One of our clients offered the following story to illustrate their understanding the Timely Feedback Model:

When I step out of the bathroom, I have somehow gotten some toilet paper stuck on my shoe. I am unaware of this. Someone who dislikes me sees me leaving the bathroom dragging toilet paper on my shoe and laughs out loud, calling me a fool for dragging the toilet paper. I feel grateful for knowing I had toilet paper on my shoe. The scolding may not have been enjoyable, nevertheless I am very happy to know that only this person saw me and that I can now correct the problem.

Let's imagine this person did not meet me coming out of the bathroom. Rather, let's say I proceed to the conference room to give a presentation to a dozen organizational leaders. As I enter the room one person points to my shoe, and I am grateful. Or perhaps no one notices. As I pace back and forth, dragging several inches of toilet paper behind me, someone within the first ten minutes may interrupt me and direct me to check my shoes. I still feel grateful and I correct my performance. What happens if no one brings this to my attention? Perhaps at the end of the day, the nicest, most polite person in the entire organization visits me in my office and says, "Please excuse me. I would like to offer you some feedback." Of course, I would respond, "Please come in."

With intensely polite and descriptive language, this person then explains that he attended my morning meeting and wanted to make a point of visiting me at the end of the day to let me know that I was dragging toilet paper during the entire meeting and around the offices all day long. He concludes by saying, "I was sure you would want to know. I am an expert at providing people with constructive, descriptive, supportive feedback. Let me know if I can ever help again." My response now is to become quite angry. He allowed me to look foolish all day. I feel embarrassed, disrespected, set up. The timing of feedback always trumps the quality of the delivery. When too much time goes by, the intent of providing feedback is felt as hostile criticism. It is felt as someone else trying to control me. It is no longer responsive to my performance, it is a thought out, calculated speech that implies the giver of the "feedback" is better, smarter, more everything than me.

When feedback is experienced within time for us to self-correct, we appreciate it, regardless of the spoken words, whether tactful or not. A feedback rich environment is a supportive communication environment. When feedback is delayed, most people tend to feel defensive. Delays in feedback occur when leaders and co-workers care more about a perfect delivery than an honest, nearly immediate response.

In an all too often seen worst case scenario, a leader may see an employee laughing out loud while speaking to another staff person on a nursing floor with patients in critical condition in the immediate vicinity. Family members and patients are somber, not jovial. Exchanging jokes on this floor is considered inappropriate by most people. Rather than walking over to the employee who is laughing, this leader wants to "get it right." He spends the day speaking with everyone who knows this employee to ask how well he takes feedback, if he gets defensive, etc. The leader then calls Human Resources to ask what kind of documentation is necessary or appropriate for a first-time offense, after all, the leader would not want to be accused of harassing this employee. The leader discusses this "case" with several people from human resources, eventually reviewing the employee's performance reviews to see if this has come up before. After all, the leader just wants to be thorough. A few days later, once fully prepared and having substantially ruined this employee's reputation with many people, the leader calls the employee into the office and says, "I would like to give you some feedback about an incident that occurred a few days ago and I need to document this meeting. Three days ago, you were seen laughing on the patient floor." In response, the employee might reply, "I have no idea what you are talking about. What is going on?" In response to the employee's blatant denial and refusal to accept either responsibility for his actions or to graciously accept this feedback, the employee is then sent to attend a training program on how to properly receive feedback.

If we need to confront employees whose performance over time is different/discrepant from the desired performance that they were hired for, we need to bring this to their attention to resolve the discrepancy, which could be attributable more to a misunderstanding than to deliberate misconduct. Either way, the leader is the "other" person in the Timely Feedback Model and it is a reasonable business practice that the leader can appropriately confront performance discrepancies. Our problem is that such an encounter does not constitute a productive and useful feedback experience. It is a review of facts, of patterns of behaviors, of reputable other people's observations. This experience is no longer self-correcting; it is other-correcting, and leaders have the right and obligation to help their employees perform at their best. Too often, performance issues that can benefit from immediate, spontaneous feedback are ignored until they become employee habits. When a leader sees someone doing something sub-optimum and says nothing, the leader is actually affirming the witnessed behavior is acceptable. We cannot not communicate. When the event is brought up later, our employees learn to stop trusting their leaders. Seeing you do something incorrectly, saying nothing, and then criticizing you a week later makes any reasonable person paranoid that, the next time the leader walks by and watches you doing your work, you'll be in trouble again at some point in the next week. The best countermeasure is to avoid being seen by the leader—leading to people hiding from their supervisors in attempts to fly below the radar.

We all benefit more from immediate feedback if something undesirable happens as opposed to reviewing the work two or three weeks later. With self-correcting feedback, time is critical. Leaders need to capitalize on when employees are most receptive to wanting to improve their performance and promote open, honest feedback among all team members.

If we miss an opportunity for being available to someone who makes a mistake, we could also use feed-forward. While some authors generally describe feed-forward as the process of previewing an event and informing or reminding someone of something he/she needs to do to be more successful the next time, we propose that the guidelines of the Timely Feedback Model still apply. The following diagram shows the opportune windows for self-correcting feedback. These are times when another person's comments/reactions are most likely to be perceived as self-correcting. Using such opportunities fosters a supportive communication climate. When the same dialogue occurs at the bottom of the trough in the diagram below, the most typical responses are defensiveness and hostility. Typically, the time when leaders feel most comfortable and confident giving what they think is feedback is in the trough, after they have taken the time to plan what they want to say. Based on our model, this is the least useful/constructive time to bring feedback to the performer's attention.

Re-Occurring Performance

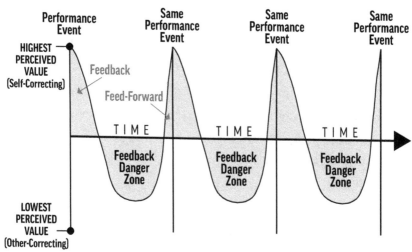

If you go through your days in a state of communication autopilot and are waiting for someone to give you feedback, or waiting for an opportunity to participate in an organization's 360-feedback process, or waiting for the annual department retreat to get feedback, you may be an unconscious communicator. Conscious communicators are constantly and consciously evaluating their communication effectiveness and both observing other's reactions as feedback and soliciting feedback when they want more. They do not wait for feedback.

Ultimately, conscious leaders engage others with purpose. To achieve any communication purpose, leaders need to learn how to monitor other's responses or feedback for evidence of grasping. Effective leaders work to increase their consciousness of the following three principles:

1. **"Feedback is self-correcting"** is a cornerstone of conscious communication.

2. **Checking for grasping** (feedback during all conversations) is part of the communication act in much the same way inhaling and exhaling are part of breathing. Using this metaphor, speaking is exhaling. Paying attention to or taking into account other's responses is like inhaling. Many people are satisfied to express themselves without giving their attention to verifying grasping. Speaking without assessing grasping is wasted breath.

3. **One-way communication inevitably fails.** One-way communication is about sending messages. These messages could be oral or electronic. No response is needed. Leader satisfaction is derived from the knowledge that the message was sent. It is tantamount to sending an employee an email while she is at lunch and going home after lunch, and then reprimanding

the employee the next day for not doing the work that was contained in the email that she never opened. This kind of message sending can make people crazy. Two-way communication refers to the dance of sending and receiving ideas, opinions, and interests. Two-way communication invites questions, back and forth. Two-way communication enables people to reply back and forth, to advance a conversation not just take turns talking. When two people take turns talking about their weekend activities, each taking turns telling their own stories—nothing is actually exchanged, no new information grasped. We have called this pattern dueling monologues.

Two-way communication is the minimum threshold for effective communication. Once experiencing two-way communication, leaders can raise the bar to actually observe their communication partners in dialogue to look for feedback that grasping is occurring. If observed, they can proceed. If not observed, they can ask questions in order to assess if grasping has occurred. If there is no feedback that grasping has occurred and if the leader does not solicit evidence that grasping is occurring in the conversation, then we are back to one-way communication in which the criteria for success is merely self-expression, not productive discourse.

Chapter Eight

Observe Your Language and Own the Impact

I f everyone engaged each other as conscious communicators we could skip this chapter. Unfortunately, only a relatively small percentage of the world population, and of leaders we have met, communicates consciously. This means that most people misinterpret others much of the time. We propose four reasons for this situation:

REASON ONE: Most people hold to and act on the popular (and incorrect) belief that messages and meaning are transmitted from senders to receivers.

THE REALITY: While we can send words to others, we cannot send meaning. Meaning is assigned by the receiver/listener. Believing otherwise leads people to conclude that, for example, if an employee does not do what I told her to do, she was either not listening, not paying attention, or otherwise failed at her responsibilities. This is a convenient but often mistaken conclusion. A more likely explanation is that the leader failed to adequately assess their grasp of the meaning she assigned to his or her message.

REASON TWO: People in positions of authority often feel that their interpretation is what matters most and that others' views are either mistaken or a distraction.

THE REALITY: Leaders' interpretation of their own communication are, in fact, much less important than how they are interpreted by others, inasmuch as these interpretations are what drives action.

REASON THREE: Many leaders think that differences in power or status have little impact on communication.

THE REALITY: We have been surprised to learn that many leaders think that their employees see them as just "one of us" and expect them to be candid in their communication with them. To the contrary, in the company of "higher-ups" who can affect their employment status and opportunities, most employees tend to avoid candid communication in fear of being judged as disloyal or ignorant. The greater the power distance, the greater the likelihood of superficial, face-saving, polite communication by the person with lower status.

REASON FOUR: We speak in rough drafts while those we speak to believe we are speaking in final draft mode.

THE REALITY: When we write something important, we can edit and rewrite it several times before it sees the light of day. When we speak, the first words we think of are often not the best ones to convey the meaning we want to express. This enables the people to whom we speak to jump to conclusions and take offense. People are often accused of saying the wrong thing even though our expressions were incomplete or in rough draft form. Alternatively, if we all acknowledged we speak in rough drafts, we could be more patient with and curious of others when they speak.

Because of these "reasons," and several other principles described in this book, speaking to others is not one of the safest things a person can do. People we speak with sometimes jump to conclusions, overreact to things they thought we said, and believe their interpretation over our intentions even when we are given a chance to explain. We live in a world where people both believe they have "buttons" that are pushable and aggressively protect this belief as a way of avoiding taking responsibility for their responses. To minimize the likelihood of this occurring, we advise people to avoid four words whose usage is most likely to be problematic. While the words themselves are not bad, they predictably evoke a negative, kneejerk reaction and hence ought be avoided. To maximize our effectiveness, conscious communicators can accept this fact of life (certain words prompt automatic responses that may have nothing to do with our intentions) and choose different words.

The next section profiles the following four trigger words:

1. "But"

2. "Why"

3. "Is"

4. "You"

In each case, we describe the challenges they present when used and provide alternative words whose use will increase your communicative effectiveness.

"BUT"

The word "but" is a conjunction used to introduce a statement that adds something to a previous statement and contrasts with it in some way. In general, a speaker begins with "but" when there is something about what they have just heard that seems problematic or incomplete, and they wish to either add new information or take exception to what has been said.

Unfortunately, utterances that begin with "but" are rarely perceived as constructive. More typically, they signal a criticism is coming, and possibly even an outright dismissal of what has been said before. It can also appear to presume a deeper knowledge of the full picture of what the original speaker was trying to express and is usually heard as hostile or dismissive.

Fortunately, there are other words that can be used to accomplish similar communicative goals. Rather than respond with "but," notice how one's thinking can change if we substitute the word "and."

I like the way you led your team through this difficult project, but you went over budget.

Or:

I like the way you led your team through this difficult project, and I am also concerned about having gone over budget.

The speaker is accomplishing much the same objective—to add a new or different perspective to the conversation—and does so in a fashion that minimizes defensiveness. Some other possible responses include "I see the situation differently" and "I have a different view of things," both of which feel additive and constructive and are less likely to create defensiveness.

"WHY"

The word "why" is an adverb used to express inquiry, asking for a reason or purpose. It can be used to obtain more information or to question a particular decision or course of action. The word "why" is one of the first questions children learn how to use. Sometimes it is because they are curious. ("Why is the sky blue?") Sometimes it is used to interrogate the motivation behind a rule or decision. ("Why do I have to go to bed now?") Again, the motives behind asking why may be quite pure. Often, though, it is not heard that way. Instead, it may be heard as an accusation.

Part of the reason that "why" can feel accusatory is because it can appear to demand a single explanation for a decision or course of action, when in fact there could be multiple motivations. Asking, "Can you describe some reasons you chose to do it that way?" will invariably produce much richer information than "Why did you do it that way?" In most cases, children learn the "why" question from their parents.

Consider that children are often repeatedly asked:
- Why didn't you finish your homework?
- Why are you watching television?
- Why don't you go out and play?
- Why didn't you get dressed?
- Why did you write on the wall?
- Why are you crying?
- Why didn't you wash the dishes?
- Why are you so slow?

When children grow and become employees and leaders, the above phrases become:
- Why are you late?
- Why did you do it that way?
- Why did you pick me?
- Why aren't you following our mission, vision, values?

You can probably tell from your own visceral reactions to this list of questions that using "why" is a risky proposition. What is meant as a request for information can often be perceived as an invasion of privacy, an invalidation of someone's experience or perspective, or an outright criticism of one's authority.

That said, the intent behind a "why" inquiry is usually good. Consider some alternative ways of getting to the same outcome without triggering defensiveness. Probably the best approach is to specifically ask for someone's reasoning, to better understand their thought process. "Why did you do that?" particularly in an annoyed or attacking tone of voice, sounds very much like "What is wrong with you? Are you stupid or crazy?" A better approach is to sincerely ask, ""How did you come to that conclusion? What was your reasoning? Tell me how you have come to think or believe that." Once again, this approach gets to the same place without putting the other person on the defense.

"IS"

The word "is" is defined as a verb, the third person singular of the verb "to be." "Is" implies a state of being rather than an action like jumping, running, or thinking.

The word "is" seems harmless. Because of the nature of language, however, the impact can be very far from harmless. "Is" works well when used in the context of concrete things (e.g., "the car is in the driveway") and less well for values or beliefs (e.g., "that applicant is qualified," or "my boss is untrustworthy").

Use of this verb in any of its forms creates an illusion of great certainty, correctness, and authority. If someone says, "*King Kong* is a great movie," the phrase takes on the quality of an assertive pronouncement rather than an expression of personal opinion. Expressing personal opinions as facts tends to challenge all who are in earshot who may have a different opinion. Once the arguments stimulated by this illusion of certainty are over, observe that nothing has been settled, people merely took time taking turns talking, and nothing has changed, including anyone's personal opinions. Imagine a considerably different conversation flow if the opening line was "I really enjoyed the movie *King Kong.*" Such a statement invites sharing and learning, not argument and winning and losing. It acknowledges that all perception is partial and makes room for learning through dialogue.

E-Prime, short for English-Prime, proposes that the verb "to be" adds little to no value in communication. Linguists who advocate for E-Prime argue that language without this verb actually clarifies thinking. Under the guidelines for E-Prime the sentence, "The film was good" cannot be stated. A speaker could say, "I liked the film." E-Prime language describes the speaker's experience rather than his/her judgment. A substantial body of linguistic work has offered additional insights into the verb "to be."

Efforts to decrease the frequency of using the verb "is" and increase personal expressions of experience increases conscious communication and productive dialogue.

There are many alternatives to the use of the word "is." Rather than saying, "The Vietnamese restaurant in my town is the best place to order Pecan Chicken," consider saying, "I like the Pecan Chicken at the Vietnamese restaurant in my town." In this way I own it. Rather than saying, "When patients are upset, using our Service Recovery Process is the best way to resolve their concerns," say, "I like using our Service Recovery Process when working with upset patients. I want you to try it too. How can I help you value it as I do?" Rather than saying, "The patient is upset," say, "When I walked into the patient's room, she started yelling at me about being hungry. I know she cannot eat because of her pending surgery. What can we do for her?"

"YOU"

The word "you" is defined as a personal pronoun. This word refers to an individual or group being addressed—singular or plural. As the meaning of this word evolves, it can also be used to refer to any person or people in general.

Once again, "you" seems harmless at first. Closer inspection reveals that it is often heard as a kind of attacking or stereotyping (as in the awful phrase "you people"). Quite often people are not at all precise when they use the word "you," leaving too much ambiguity about who is actually being addressed. Moreover, "you" is sometimes used when the intent is to shift responsibility or blame from oneself to others.

The use of the pronoun "I" creates ownership and suggests personal responsibility. Saying "I need to exercise more often" is a personal statement and even a public commitment. Some people prefer to say, "You just know when you need to exercise more often. You know what I mean?" In this statement, no responsibility is owned. In speaking like this we take a personal pronoun and turn it into an indefinite pronoun—using the word "you" rather than "some people," as in "when someone needs to …" and "most people could benefit from …" Using the word "you" as an indefinite pronoun dilutes personal responsibility. One of our favorite expressions is "The problem in this organization is you have to do more to increase accountability." When everyone says, "You need to increase accountability," no one does it. In our travels, we have yet to hear, "I need to improve my accountability."

The word "you" is also challenging because it (like "is") presumes certainty on the part of the speaker, such as "You need to speak up" (as opposed to "I need to listen better") or "You need to improve your customer service image" (as opposed to "I need to find a way to help you improve your customer service").

Even when telling phone customers that they need to fill out paperwork or take actions needed to expedite a product return or improve an outcome, beginning with "You need to …" usually creates defensiveness and resistance. The word "you" is a push. Alternately, a sales associate could say "Thank you for your call. I want to replace your defective merchandise. I need you to fill out the warranty card so that I can help you."

As long as I am saying, "You need to or you should" when I really mean to be saying, "I need to or I should," I am committing an act of "disownership," and you are conspiring with me to help prevent me from owning my personal responsibilities. When we communicate like this with each other we coconspire to minimize if not eliminate any accountabilities between us.

There are alternatives. Using the word "I" rather than using the word "you" is an act of personal responsibility and accountability. The word "you" is, therefore, best always used as a definite pronoun. It means you, the person I am speaking to. Using the word "you" as an indefinite pronoun, as a substitute for the phrases "some people," "some groups of people," or "when some people," tends to diminish mutual accountability and personal responsibility.

As one of my colleagues once told me, "I would like to review some material on conflict management. You know when you feel exhausted from a day's work and you head to your favorite pub for a few beers, and just as you are starting to feel better, the bartender starts giving you a hard time …" I interrupted him and said, "Excuse me, I do not feel exhausted from a day's work; I feel energized. At the end of the day, I usually go home to my family. The people I socialize with do not give me a hard time. If you want to talk about your personal conflict, own it. Begin all over again using the word 'I' rather than 'you.'"

In summary, most people are unconscious about their use of all four of these words. We use them mainly with good intent, though they often trigger negative and defensive reactions which could better be avoided. When tensions increase, when people feel vulnerable, and when conversations become heated, these are times the negative impact of using these words increases dramatically. Under such circumstances, use of these four words can easily erode meaningful dialogue and severely compromise productivity. When speaking with others, rather than attempt to assess if the tension is too high to use these problematic words, we believe the best course of action is to work at minimizing our use of these words. They are usually not helpful.

A few months ago, I was working with a client who was a newly promoted director of a critical department in her organization. She earned an excellent reputation as a manager yet needed to be persuaded to take the director position. Of all the candidates, internal and external, she was clearly the most qualified. As part of the promotion, the hiring vice president proposed that the new director could benefit from a personal coach to help her overcome some of her anxieties about the new leadership position.

During our initial assessment, surprisingly, she demonstrated a marked tendency to subtly argue with the consultant. I would propose something, and she would respond, "Good idea, but ..." Typically, during a first session with a client I tactfully work to increase my client's awareness about just one or two of his/her behaviors. I chose to bring the word "but" to this person's attention. Her response was that she never uses the word. She was not lying; her use of this word had become habitual and hence unconscious. To help her understand

and feel the problems that can arise when people overuse the word "but," I began "butting" everything she said. She quickly realized this word does not help improve productive dialogue. We then agreed on two homework assignments.

- The next time she attends someone else's business meeting, discreetly count the number of "buts" spoken, and by whom.

- The next time she has a one-on-one with her staff, try to summarize what they talk about before answering an employee's question or saying the word "but."

At our next meeting, she said that she was amazed at how many times people cut each other off with the word "but" before getting a more complete idea about each other's points and concerns. She also reported that her employees really appreciated her checking in with them to better understand their issues/concerns. Essentially, she learned to see "buts" (i.e., bring them into discursive consciousness), and she learned about the power of paraphrasing. She still needed to learn to decrease her own use of the word "but." We practiced a "no 'but' rule" during the remainder of our meeting, and realized she continued to have no awareness of her own use of this word. Her next homework assignment was to ask a colleague for help. I wanted her to ask someone she trusted to count her "buts" during meetings that she managed for the department. Several meetings later, this director was cured of "but."

Changing behavior is difficult. We must first become conscious of what our own behavior is and then become conscious of better ways of communicating. We must come to believe that we have the ability to change, and moreover that the benefit of changing our behavior is worth the trouble of learning both about ourselves and new ways to communicate This takes time and usually involves enlisting a partner who can accelerate learning and feedback.

In one organization, a hospital in eastern Massachusetts, a senior vice president required a large number of employees to participate in mandatory training on a specific subject. The good news was that people actually wanted this training opportunity. When five people did not show up for one of the required programs, they were sent an email, copied to all of them, demanding they explain why they did not attend the program on that day. One of the employees (an organizational leader) responded apologetically explaining that her children had been very sick for several days and that her husband was out of town caring for another very ill relative. Her response was personal, private information that no one had a right to know. She had legitimately taken the day off using her accrued time. The "why" question presumed the absence was disrespectful. In truth, this mother had another priority that day. When she hit the reply button to her email she accidentally hit "reply all," and the message was broadcast to many people who had no need or right to this information. She felt scolded, reprimanded and threatened. The senior vice president who sent that original email is a wonderful, compassionate leader; by putting the word "why" in print, the SVP had no control over how it could be received. A better original email could have been, "I am sorry you missed today's program. I hope you are OK. Please contact my assistant within the next couple of weeks so that we can reschedule this session for you. Thank you."

We all have choices about the words we use, especially when we are conscious of options. The habitual use of the words "but," "why," "you," and "is" linguistically lead to pontifications, not engagement. Effective leaders need to work toward a language of engagement. When we are not conscious, we can cause harm, disrespect, poor quality work, disengagement, and other organizational problems without realizing our own contribution to these outcomes. What we have learned in our lives thus far has gotten us here. To get to the next plateau of leadership effectiveness, we can learn how to become more conscious, more aware, and more effective. To strengthen these word choice options/skills, we strongly recommend that *you* (written here as a personal pronoun) work with a partner who can provide you with daily feedback as you work to eliminate these words from your vocabulary. While they may work some of the time, we know they do not work all of the time. We invite you to raise the bar on your conscious word choices.

PART FOUR

Building the Conscious Organization

CHAPTER NINE

Conscious Communication in Teams

T hus far this book has focused on the effectiveness of the individual leader, who through more conscious communication can improve both their personal and their organization's effectiveness. Conscious leaders understand the importance of articulating clear goals, of communicating those goals *and* of checking for grasping. Conscious leaders pay attention to and when necessary provide feedback in real time to allow for self-correction and improvement. Conscious leaders—and conscious communicators more generally—are deeply self-aware and know what they do not know.

Fortunately, leaders never work alone (the word itself implies a group of willing followers) and each day presents myriad opportunities to solicit and learn from others' perspectives. Most work in contemporary organizations is expressly interdisciplinary and team based, whether we are talking about manufacturing, engineering, hospitality, or health care. For this reason, there is nothing more valuable to a leader than an engaged and well-informed team.

Unfortunately, we have personally experienced and worked with many teams that fail to live up to this potential. While the research is clear that diverse teams are consistently more effective than homogenous ones, *many* leaders—perhaps for fear of "losing control"—are either unwilling or unable to form teams that represent diverse perspectives or to create the kind of open dialogue that takes full advantage of this diversity. Instead, they are often first and last to speak in team meetings, do most of the talking, and argue with alternative perspectives when offered (and over time, once team members see how their perspectives are received, they stop offering them). They may also be conflict averse and quickly shut down or "take offline" all differences of opinion which if handled differently could lead to constructive and creative thinking.

Recently, one of the largest and most influential companies in the world—Google—mounted a vast and historic study of what makes teams effective. This research study—dubbed the Aristotle Project—aimed to identify what separated high-performing teams from their less effective counterparts. The investigators approached the project with the hypothesis that smart people made for smart teams, but their findings showed that this was not at all the case. Teams of bright individual "all stars" struggled to communicate and to coalesce. On the other hand, teams wherein members felt a deep sense of *psychological safety*—in which they were encouraged to freely share their ideas and perspective with others—were by far the best performing. In fact, while other dimensions mattered somewhat, psychological safety was the only factor that characterized *all* high-performing teams.

Expressed in the vocabulary of this book, the ability of a team to be collectively conscious of the communication environment they are creating and sustaining is equivalent to psychological safety. Knowing that one's ideas matter and are taken seriously by others has many positive consequences: increased employee engagement and motivation; better solutions as a result of brainstorming; and problem-solving with the benefit of multiple diverse perspectives.

Economist Scott Page makes a similar point in his work on the "diversity bonus." He goes beyond considering the social or moral value of inclusion to empirically demonstrate when diverse team members are encouraged to participate the team is unequivocally better at solving challenging problems. We have made the argument in this book that conscious communicators are both highly self-aware and attentive to how others will receive and make sense of their communication. Applied to teams, the same general approach applies.

INDIVIDUAL VERSUS TEAM PERFORMANCE: THE PROBLEM OF MIXED MESSAGES

Given that the research on effective teams is so clear, why do most teams struggle? One reason has to do with the limitations we have been discussing throughout this book, which also appear in the relationship between a leader and his or her team. On one end of the continuum are team leaders who are narcissistic, believe they are smarter than anyone on their team, could not care less about what others think or believe, and hence treat their team members solely with regard to their ability to effectively implement or execute their "nonnegotiable" directives. In this example, team members are likely disengaged, fearful, or unwilling to speak up and may even be seeking other employment. At the same time, this type of team "leader" has no interest in adapting his or her communication to individual needs or interest, never checks for grasping, and may be unaware of how negatively he or she is perceived.

At the other end of the continuum lies leaders who are deeply aware of their limitations and value their team members specifically because they bring diverse perspectives outside of his or her awareness. They rely on their teams completely not only for execution but also as *thinking partners in a carefully crafted atmosphere of psychological safety.* They purposefully design and monitor their communication to ensure that team members are grasping their intent and make adjustments to ensure mutual understanding and a positive work environment. They ask for feedback and sincerely welcome being challenged. More than likely they are aware of how they are perceived by team members and are constantly seeking and soliciting feedback about how they might develop and improve.

As you have no doubt experienced, all leaders fall somewhere along this continuum, and their general attitude toward their teams shows up in myriad ways: In how members are chosen, developed, and retained; in how meetings are scheduled, planned, and run; and in how the team communicates to others outside of the team, both in and outside of the company. Being a member of a high-performing team with a conscious leader can feel like a memorable peak experience that shapes one's life and career. Being a member of a dysfunctional team with an ineffective, self-involved leader can feel like a soul-destroying, never-ending ordeal.

Another reason that teams struggle has less to do with the individual limitations of team leaders and more to do with the focus on individual achievement that underlies much of Western culture. Despite the fact that we may recognize in principle that "individual" actions are socially situated and motivated, most of us remain determined to assign both credit and blame to individuals. In an increasingly interdisciplinary and connected world, this habit creates problems. What may look like individual accomplishments or mistakes are in many if not most circumstances the result of a long chain of actions by many people.

Research into medical error reveal that focusing on individual performance (positive or negative) inevitably leads us to miss the big picture. The same is true with teams. If we want teams to be high performing, we must commit to measuring the success of the team's outcomes as a unit, not simply by the success of its constituent members. Maintaining a focus on individual performance while simultaneously only celebrating individual success can work against team effectiveness.

Sports teams underscore these points. Time and again, teams find that they cannot reach their full potential when they organize around the success of a single superstar. Effective team leaders must promote both individual performance and also team goals that are shared by all members of the team. In his wonderful book about team dysfunction, Patrick Lencioni concludes that great teams hit their stride when they *discover a shared aspiration that unifies all of their previously siloed efforts.* Teams don't do well with mixed and conflicting messages. If individual performance is all that matters, then say so. But if you aspire to *team* effectiveness, be certain to encourage, measure and celebrate *team* achievements.

THINKING VERSUS HAVING THOUGHTS; BEING VERSUS PERFORMING CONSCIOUS COMMUNICATION

In his extraordinary work on the power of dialogue, physicist David Bohm made a crucial distinction between "having thoughts," which is the uncritical repetition of ideas that exist in the environment, and "thinking" which involves exposing those ideas to logic and analysis before expressing them as one's own. In the classroom, we quite often hear students repeat what they have heard and uncritically accepted from the media or their friends and families. When asked to reflect on why they hold these beliefs and on how they came to them, they have nothing to say because they have not done that work. Their superficial engagement with ideas drawn from the cultural zeitgeist has the appearance of thinking, yet there isn't much there.

Unfortunately, many people in leadership positions do a similar thing when it comes to working with teams. Just as we all know that a diet of junk food is bad for our health, many if not most people also know in theory what good communication should look like and how a well-performing team ought to function. Simply knowing how it should look versus making it a reality is the difference between watching sports on television and going to the gym! One is an empty performance; the other is a disciplined commitment. Unfortunately, many teams are run by people who either don't want to fully engage with members (and if you believe you know all the answers, why bother?) or who want to but do not know how to do so. There just are not very many great models to follow, and much of this information is still not central in management education.

Two humorous stories we experienced drive home the point. The first involved a frustrated aerospace executive who was under pressure from his superiors to make a decision while his direct reports were not unified in their ideas about what to do. In his frustration, he met with his team and with anger in his voice implored them: "I want consensus, and I want it now, dammit." The second example was from the general manager of a California utility who had received some feedback that he should be more open to feedback. In his annual employee address, he intoned that he "now had an open-door policy, that anyone could come to see me," but then continued that "you had better have a darn good reason." In both cases, the leader understood that something different was expected of them but either couldn't or didn't know how to do what was needed to sincerely make the change.

Parallel to the points we made in chapter one, the first step toward improved communication is to admit to knowing what you do not know; to shift oneself out of the starring role to allow others into the spotlight; and to begin to create a communication environment where people feel safe and sincerely invited to share their ideas and perspectives. Doing so takes humility and discipline, and over time the learned ability to guide the conversation from within rather than dictate what is discussed from above. But as Google and Page and Lencioni and many others have clearly shown, laying down a foundation of psychological safety and trust has numerous game-changing benefits for employee well-being and team performance.

Conscious communicators are fully aware that the words they use are intended to approximate much more complex ideas. They appreciate that the spoken word is imperfect; it is ambiguous; it is an attempt to share a concept or image in one's mind. Conscious communicators are more aware of the limitations of speech and language than are others. They give each other latitude with their expressions, they respect each other. They are patient. They see each other's expressions as rough drafts with more to come rather than as definitive statements subject to agreement or disagreement. Conscious communicators foster a supportive environment, a supportive communication climate. Conscious communicators demonstrate that clarity is negotiated, not commanded; that assignments are explored and benefit from challenging questions; that meaning is always assigned by the receiver not dictated by the speaker; that they have a greater impact on others because of what they model than what they say; and that organizational success depends upon the success of every single employee. Leaders who learn conscious communication engage in constant calibration with the members of their team. They know they can only see part of the picture and they respectfully appreciate the contributions each member of the team can make to enlarge each other's view, to be able to see more than any one leader can possibly envision.

Put differently, autocratic, narcissistic leaders hurt themselves because they limit their access to new information and perspectives that could expand their understanding of the situation. We (Eric) worked with a manufacturing organization in California whose CEO was known by his employees as the "little general." Over a long period of time, his senior leaders had come to realize that the only ideas he supported were his own and therefore had stopped trying to offer anything new. In working with this leadership team at a management retreat, I was surprised when he kicked off the session declaring that one of his long-standing employees, Bill, needed to be terminated. Apparently, Bill was beloved by some on the team, and they could no longer hold their tongues—they spoke immediately and with passion about how valuable he was to the organization. Sensing a disagreement that was evolving into a screaming match, as facilitator I used the principles of dialogue to de-escalate the situation and help the team discover the power of dialogue and multiple perspectives.

I went around the table and asked each attendee to speak only about their direct experience with Bill as a colleague and employee. The CEO went first, relating two especially embarrassing interactions he had with Bill in the presence of important customers. Next a vice president explained that Bill had been his mentor when he first came to the company, and that his support was invaluable. A third person spoke about Bill's ability to work across silos, and so on. After everyone had had a chance to speak, I re-posed the initial question: Should Bill be let go? But now everyone—including the CEO!—recognized that the decision was more nuanced than anyone had initially thought. Bill was clearly in the wrong job, but with the proper duties and coaching could continue to play a key role at the company. The lesson to the team was also clear—making room for multiple perspectives leads to better decisions.

There is another advantage of conscious team communication that features a different benefit of psychological safety and a supportive communication climate, the ability to provide honest and constructive feedback without fear of negative repercussions. Earlier in this book we discussed the notion of feedback in depth and made the point that people learn best when they receive feedback in a naturally occurring and timely fashion, where at all possible directly from work processes and not requiring scheduled conversation. Additionally, there is another kind of honest feedback that can occur in work teams that can be incredibly helpful in members' ongoing development: a safe environment in which people can tell each other what they are doing that helps the team and what they are doing which gets in the way.

Based on our experience, we predict that few of you have ever been on a team where this kind of honesty was encouraged or even possible. The more usual pattern is to avoid or enable poor performance until the problem becomes too big to ignore. Doing so deprives our colleagues and even our team leader of important opportunities to learn. A client health care system recently presented us with a challenge which at first appeared straightforward. They were interested in a referral to an expert who could work with physicians for whom English was their second language and their primary language accent severely compromised how much their patients were able to understand their instructions. Concerns and complaints about poor communication had been escalating for nearly two years. The problems of poor communication, largely flowing from an inability to speak in a way that was easily intelligible to patients, were eventually elevated to a senior leader, who, in turn, accepted *responsibility* for solving the problem.

Nevertheless, whose problem is this really? Perhaps some of the problem belonged to the patients who were not patient enough to work with and understand the physicians. Maybe the problem belonged to the immediate supervisor. The tentative plan was to pay a speech pathologist to help each physician, if any of them wanted the assistance. Approximately 35 of the 150 physicians were categorized as having substantial communication problems because of their accents. The organization, by proxy of the department head, became responsible for the physician's success—not the individual physicians.

We asked the supervisor of these 150 physicians how the 35 were treated by their colleagues. "Most people do not understand them, so they essentially avoid having to work with them." Our next question was, "When physicians with heavy and nearly unintelligible accents speak up at meetings, care teams, or during rounding, what do their colleagues do to help them?" The answer? "Well, nothing. It is not their responsibility. Besides, it would be rude for a physician to criticize a colleague." Essentially, *all* of the coworking physicians, nurses, midlevel providers, office staff, and administrators who interacted with the 35 physicians who were very difficult to understand unwittingly participated in an *unconscious conspiracy to deny all opportunities for constructive feedback.* As a result of this conspiracy, the problem is continuing to worsen.

When did helping an individual to be more effective in his/her work become rude or criticizing behavior? We were offered a crystal-clear example of a work group fully unconscious about their communication and about the implications of this unconsciousness on the organization and its patients. Conscious communicators value timely feedback, understand their responses will be interpreted as helpful, and appreciate all efforts to improve communication effectiveness. Unconscious communicators live in a world protecting their self-image at all costs and perceive opportunities to expand their awareness as threats to their own narrow perceptions of themselves. Teams and workgroups led by unconscious leaders are substantially compromised because of the difficulties of both carrying one's self-image around and protecting it from all threats that could show us we do not know everything. Protecting who we think we are usually prevents us from discovering our full leadership potential. Every action that we do not take to improve someone's performance is an action to prevent his or her improvement.

Organizations form teams to solve challenges that transcend individual efforts, and leaders are charged to guide teams in their attempts to address these challenges. What we have shown here is that individuals chosen for these leadership roles approach the situation very differently. In our experience, the most successful leaders help define the problem for their teams and *do not assume in advance that they know the answer*; instead, they cultivate a safe and inclusive communication environment which enables members to suggest possible solutions that build upon one another. Moreover, and consistent with the idea of psychological safety, they further encourage team members to conduct small experiments with different approaches to garner more information about what solutions may or may not work.

> *The most successful leaders help define the problem for their teams and do not assume in advance that they know the answer.*

We hope that you see this chapter as building upon the earlier ones, inasmuch as we are encouraging you to first take a hard look at yourself as a communicator, then examine how you are seen by others close to you, and how your communication style is regarded by the teams that you lead. In every case, the principles are much the same. Be honest about your weaknesses, solicit honest feedback, and continue to grow and develop.

CHAPTER TEN

Scaling Up: Creating a Conscious Culture

A s consultants and experts advising organizations in trouble, we have often been approached by someone in senior management who was convinced that their organization's problems were "cultural" and could be easily fixed if only we could "install" a new culture. Students of anthropology will immediately see the problem with this—culture evolves organically over time and is notoriously hard to change. That said, our response to these individuals was usually heard as less than comforting. We asked them, "If you don't like your current culture, for what possible reason do you and your colleagues choose to re-create it each and every day?"

We began this book by stating that an unwillingness to look in the mirror is a deal breaker when it comes to making improvements. *The same is true for the enterprise as a whole.* For individuals to make meaningful and lasting improvements in their lives, looking in the mirror and realizing their contribution to their present situation is a powerful starting place. One of the greatest obstacles to lasting organizational change is the unwillingness of managers and employees to acknowledge the true nature of their current reality and their active role in continually reproducing all of the things they claim to hate. While on the face of it, it seems illogical that people would continue to perpetuate a dysfunctional system, in fact there can be many reasons for this. For example, while professing a need for change, people may be frightened of whether or not their skills will still be needed in a transformed organization. Alternatively, people may profess a need for change publicly but privately acknowledge the benefits they reap from the status quo.

The idea of psychological safety that Google discovered to be so key to effective teamwork is equally powerful when applied to culture. Think about your current organization. Which topics are permissible to discuss, and which are off limits to even respectful exploration? Sometimes called "elephants in the room" or "sacred cows," these verboten subjects say a lot about an organization's culture particularly with regard to communication. When some things become undiscussable, they do not disappear. Rather, they go underground. The result is that ideas and practices that could be improved by being challenged and discussed remain in place despite the fact that many, if not most, people do not support them. Respectful challenges and naming of sacred cows are met in these organizations by censure and even dismissal, sending a clear message to others that further input is unwelcome, effectively depriving the leadership of diverse perspectives that we know lead to better decision-making.

Many organizations today engage in attempts to profess and practice a values-based leadership style that emphasizes respect for employees, customers, patients, and vendors. For some organizations, values such as integrity, trust, and collaboration are integrated throughout the official vocabulary of the organization. Unfortunately, there can be a huge chasm between the "expressed" culture—what the organization could be or wants to be—and the actual culture. All too often, even in cultures that declare themselves as valuing trust and communication, the perception that an individual was insubordinate to a senior leader can result in immediate dismissal. Even providing what feels like authentic feedback to a leader can result in dismissal for "no longer being a good fit" for the organization. Of course, when this happens, the word quickly spreads and others conclude that regardless of the "party line," loyalty and following the hierarchy are the true values of the organization. Truth, honesty, and authenticity nearly always come in very low in such cultures. The culture reflects what people actually do, not what they preach.

In an organization in which leaders have become conscious communicators, respectful challenges to current practices are invited and welcomed as potential sources of new information. The challenge, however stated, is perceived as an invitation to explore, not a win-lose situation. When such an invitation is extended, leaders who do *not* understand conscious communication tend to perceive divergent opinions as a threat to the status quo. The emerging discussion, if permitted to occur, frequently digresses into a "which side are you on" mentality, as if there were only two sides. During such discussions, when one person is speaking the other tends to be mentally rehearsing arguments to fire back as soon as the first person takes a breath. Speech patterns contain an abundance of

- "why" questions (Why do you think that way, you idiot?),

- "but" responses (but we can't, but you do not understand, but you forgot to …), and

- "is" statements as each person attempts to create and defend his/her own perspective on reality.

A leader who is conscious of communication might respond with "Thanks for the question. Let's explore what you are bringing up" in an effort to expand their world view and understanding of the issues. In addition to their speech patterns containing relatively few "why," "but," and "is" phrases, there is also paraphrasing ("So if I understand you correctly, you said …") and mutual pursuit of understanding ("Please help me understand what you mean …") Leading this way requires people to differentiate between discussion—where opposing ideas battle against each other and employees are encouraged to either agree or disagree with points made—and dialogue, which allows people to create new, compelling solutions that draw upon multiple perspectives.

None of this is meant to suggest that there will not be times when leaders will have to act unilaterally based upon their best judgment. However, this approach to leadership communication suggests that if a leader knows in advance that there is limited opportunity for input, he or she should make that clear up front as a way of managing expectations. The good news is that no employee has the idea that their perspective should carry the day every time they are asked for input. Instead, both leaders and employees benefit when there is a healthy balance between engaged dialogue and decisive decision-making when it is called for.

One of the challenges leaders face in encouraging dialogue is the learned tendency of many if not most cultures to turn *difference into opposition*. Imagine a team seeking to understand a recent downturn in business; manufacturing may attribute it to a problem with design; engineering may see it as a problem with sales. All too often, these viewpoints become pitted against each other and the conversation becomes focused on determining which idea is *right*, when in reality, they could *all* be viable! Much like the proverbial blind men and the elephant, different individuals see different sides of a problem, and the power of dialogue is the ability to talk in ways that allow multiple perspectives to coexist, complement, and build upon one another in the service of innovation and more complex solutions.

Please note we are not proposing that all problems can be resolved in one conversation by calling it dialogue rather than discussion. We do believe a culture of dialogue is more authentic and successful than one of discussion. The example offered above, that of an employee respectfully challenging a practice or idea, can take place in an unsafe culture or in one of psychology safety. In an unsafe culture, there will be pressure to tightly control the discussion, to establish right and wrong, and to contain or limit the time for the discussion. The discussion, or question itself, will be seen as disruptive and awkward. The goal of the leader who does not value dialogue is to get back to work and get closure on this disruption as quickly as possible. There would appear to be no appreciation for the concept of strategic ambiguity or the value of further exploration, of potentially inviting others into the dialogue, of suspending judgment in favor of thoughtful reflection. When done well, dialogue is a practice of open communication—engaging others with a nonjudgmental stance open to new learning and new possibilities.

One of us spent some time working with a large insurance company as they struggled to survive a particularly active hurricane season, with anticipated claims that could have bankrupted the company. Since this level of damage was almost unprecedented, no one had reliable past experience from which to draw. Consequently, the conversations among senior leaders were necessarily exploratory. I worked closely with the senior executive in the region to reinforce his natural positive tendency—to encourage open dialogue and competing perspectives. In so doing, I observed something wonderful which has stayed with me. At one point in the conversation, the senior team became excited about a particular course of action, moving quickly from exploration to planning. The senior executive, sensing that everyone had not yet had a chance to weigh in, purposefully slowed the process down by saying, "Let's not finish cooking this yet. Let's keep stirring the pot for a while and see what comes up before we make a final plan." Some important new ideas emerged as a result.

Another reason that psychological safety and open communication is key to a supportive communication culture is that all organizations are living systems, and as such are extremely sensitive to blockages. Life circulates—in your body, blockages of air or blood are catastrophic for the survival of the organism. In organizations, blockages of information lead to siloed and suboptimal decision-making. One famous example can be found in the *Challenger* disaster, where the space shuttle exploded, and all of the crew perished. The cause of the explosion was a defective O-ring that didn't function properly at low temperatures. Postmortem analysis revealed that a number of employees at NASA and its subcontractors were aware of this potential vulnerability and even tried to communicate it "up the chain" but were impeded by a culture that increasingly placed cost and schedule over safety concerns. This example clearly shows that there can be negative and even tragic consequences to cultures that support blockages in communication.

Life circulates, and intelligence is distributed in all living systems. Even in your body, while stomach and lung cells do not have language, they are intelligent in that they continually make things work and keep you alive. Conversely, there are many things that your brain does not know how to do in language but does anyway. You know how to pump your blood and digest your food because the intelligence for doing so is distributed throughout your body. Even your emotional intelligence works with the conscious, subconscious, and numerous bodily functions to support your awareness and help you manage stress and adventures throughout the day.

Similarly, intelligence in every organization is distributed through every function, level, and specialty. Conscious communicators understand that their main job is not to develop solutions on their own. Rather, they work to *create opportunities for ideas and solutions to emerge from those who are doing the work and likely know it best*. Leadership has its own unique perspective to bring to these conversations—they can better see the enterprise view, the environment, and possibilities for collaboration across the organization. But this is only one perspective among many, which is a major reason that great leaders are more like orchestra conductors than individual players.

The same insurance executive mentioned above taught me an important lesson along these lines that I continue to practice. He explained that he had always been a "quick study" and invariably came into meetings with proposed solutions in his mind. He had learned, however, that if he refrained from speaking and sharing his ideas for ten to fifteen minutes, that (1) those very same ideas would be introduced by others, who may just take longer to get there; and (2) ideas that emerged from the team were more enthusiastically supported than solutions he would impose at the start.

Moreover, in attempting to create open, safe, collaborative communication environments, leaders are challenged by the categories and structures that have been created over time to manage the work and complexity of the present organization. Departments organized by function are the biggest obstacle in some cases, wherein employee loyalty to a particular group, specialty or perspective makes them unable to collaborate and see a bigger or different picture. In this case, leaders can experiment with building agile, interdisciplinary networks of employees that cut across levels and departments and thereby create new pathways for information to circulate. Human resource professionals can encourage enterprise thinking and heedful interrelating by how they orient new employees to their work. Increasingly organizations are responding to wicked environmental and strategic challenges by forming ad hoc SWAT teams and temporary agile networks to develop breakthrough solutions that reflect the organization as a whole.

Organizations are organic, not static systems. Conscious organizations build in rewards for constant calibration, monitoring success, and ongoing conversation management. Conscious organizations do not wait for periodic "oil changes" according to a prescribed calendar. They do not wait for annual performance reviews to raise the bar on performance. Rather, conscious organizations are fluid, continuously adapting to changing customer needs, and constantly tuned into employees, customers, and the community. The organization is not a machine to be tuned up once a year. Conscious organizations function more as ecosystems than machines.

Leadership is a team sport. Leading and shaping culture is accomplished less by control and more by inspiration and collaboration. Leadership in a conscious organization is shared. Leadership is joyfully distributed to people with appropriate expertise and not limited to those with "appropriate" titles.

An organization led by people who are conscious of how communication actually functions looks dramatically different from organizations that are locked into older, long disproven communication theories. Leaders in many organizations today continue to believe that leaders know best and that communication breakdowns are always the fault of the receiver for not listening well enough. In conscious organizations, leaders work hard at stopping some poor practices and increasing more effective communication practices:

LEADERS STOP DOING THIS	LEADERS START DOING THIS
1. Cascading strategic goals via formal presentations, agendas, and talking points though hierarchal levels.	Establishing strategic goals then engaging groups across diverse levels to have meaningful conversations about how to best accomplish them.
2. Holding formal monthly meetings during which key leaders read PowerPoint presentations to middle management.	Facilitating engagement meetings to listen to and learn from the experiences of middle management and below in trying to execute on the strategy.
3. Holding the HR training and development function responsible for employees' performance and alignment with cultural values.	Holding each leader responsible for ensuring that they and their teams behave in ways that are consistent with organizational values and culture. Human Resources can be supportive in this effort but should not own it, since doing so can create conflict between the desired culture and how people actually behave.
4. Emphasizing annual performance reviews.	Emphasizing the responsibility of all leaders to enable all employees to have timely access to performance improving/sustaining feedback, at least daily. The annual review is merely a summary of performance improvement opportunities throughout the year. In and of itself, a performance review is not a performance improvement process.
5. Asking, "What can we do to make employees more accountable?"	Asking, "What can I do as a leader to be more accountable?"
6. Punishing disruptive thinkers.	Becoming more curious and less judgmental when invited to learn about other perspectives.

SHAPING A CONSCIOUS CULTURE– CONSCIOUSLY

As stated above, culture change is impossible unless one first has a clear understanding of the current reality, of the values, assumptions, and practices that characterize your organization today. We believe that such awareness of an organization's culture or ecosystem is so complex, no one individual can ever be fully aware of all the components and interrelationships. Culture change is a team effort. Leaders who seek to make change without first discerning and establishing a common understanding of *current* reality are destined to fail because their suggestions will not be seen as credible to employees. Attempting to move toward a future state without understanding how we are maintaining (enabling, propping up) the current state guarantees long term failure. Culture change is especially problematic if the existing culture puts loyalty ahead of honesty. When people fear for their jobs, truth is typically one of the first casualties. If no one can publicly disagree with the leader, any attempt to improve the organization's culture or ecosystem is an illusion. Inevitably, because of leadership not knowing what they do not know and employees who live with the day-to-day fear of what can happen (and has happened) if they do not sing the praises of their leaders, some flurry of activity will take place and leaders will announce positive superficial culture change results while the genuine concerns of the employees and the organization as a whole get woven deeper and deeper into the fabric of the organization. All are expected to support the illusion of a culture change or be labeled disloyal. New leaders will be promoted or hired to the extent that they support the latest illusions. When the senior leadership turns over, the new leader will begin a new culture change initiative. This scenario has played out hundreds of times when leaders have been sent from corporate headquarters to make change in a local office only to find tremendous resistance and even sabotage. Each cycle increases the resistance to real change. These periodic culture change cycles have contributed to an expression many employees are too familiar with—flavor of the month. Conversely, once you have engaged in honest, authentic dialogue grounded in reality, the possibility of making something new, different, organic, and sustainable can emerge.

Experience has taught us that organizational culture is highly organic and cannot be *managed* in any known sense of the word. Instead, it can be cultivated like a garden, and with any luck over time it will begin to look different. The most important factors that define and sustain an organizational culture are the conversations that take place during the day-to-day ritual practices and the conversations through which employees perceive the organization's rewards and punishments.

In the organizational context, there are many long-standing rituals that can provide clues that reveal aspects of the culture. Ritual practices can be anything from how parking spaces are assigned to the nature of standing meetings (topics, attendance, frequency) to the structure of holiday parties. Culture can be shaped by eliminating certain practices and adding others, and if the new practices are followed with consistency, they will eventually "stick." Rewards and punishments refer to both formal compensation and benefits and the sources of and reasons for informal recognition or informal censure. Generally speaking, employee understanding of rewards and punishment circulates in every organization in the form of often told stories, the morals of each are meant to communicate to new members and outsiders what the organization truly values.

When an individual (leader or coworker) who is conscious of

how communication works compliments an employee, that employee feels recognized, respected, and appreciated. When an individual who is clueless about how communication works gives a compliment to an employee, that employee often feels patronized, embarrassed, anxiously waiting for the other "shoe to fall," or even curious about what is really going on.

If there is a discrepancy between an employee's actual and desired performance, a person who understands conscious communication could ask ,"Are you OK?" as a first question. Someone with little or no understanding of how communication works might ask, "Why are you making so many mistakes this week?"

Culture is shaped in every interaction, every conversation. Culture change occurs as the number of leaders and employees within an organization reach a critical mass of individuals who understand how communication works and who use their knowledge to improve all of their conversations. As they become more effective, so too does the entire organization.

Regardless of educational background, human beings are perceptive at seeing through empty organizational rhetoric to assess what the organization really cares about. No amount of talking will dissuade people from orienting themselves to their coworkers' experiences of the established practices of formal and informal recognition and punishment. Hence shaping culture requires a hard look at existing rewards, recognition, and punishments to see how well they align with the desired culture.

One of the most important changes that has occurred over time in organizational C-suites—the top executives who "run" the business—is that their membership has often been expanded to include the chief information officer, the chief human resources officer, and the chief communication officer (although they are called by various and creative names). These individuals are responsible for recruiting and supporting the people in the organization and providing them with the tools they need to be effective. Before these voices were present in senior leadership, many top executives treated communication and technology as afterthoughts that could be ignored or taken for granted. Today, many CIOs and senior VPs of HR and communication are strong advocates for the kinds of communication and culture change that we have been promoting throughout this book: practices that encourage information sharing, collaboration, continuous learning and development, and employee engagement in decision-making. As such, conscious communication both supports these practices and is the methodology for establishing these practices.

At this point, you may be seeing a thread that connects conscious leadership with conscious teamwork and the conscious organization. Depending on where you are positioned in your organization—and on the nature of your organization's current reality when it comes to culture—you will have more or less agency in driving toward this change. The stark reality is that great communicators sometimes find themselves unable to succeed in organizations that value gossip and that permit "sacred cows" to persist. If, however, you are situated in a way that allows you to influence communication in a small team or unit, your work can have a positive impact on the organization as a whole as people begin to experience—and tell colleagues about—the many benefits of conscious communication.

CHAPTER ELEVEN

Putting It All Together–Integrity, Vulnerability, and Humility

We began this book with the assertion that leadership development is impossible without honest self-assessment of how one is communicating today. In this chapter we return to the role of the individual. Our focus here is to clearly spell out the qualities to which every great leader/communicator ought to aspire: integrity, vulnerability, and humility.

INTEGRITY

Perhaps the greatest disconnect that we observe in promoting leadership development is between people's self-perceptions and how they are perceived by others. In part, this is a manifestation of the fundamental theme of this book—lack of conscious awareness of how we appear to others—but this gap can also result from a lack of integrity.

People with integrity are committed to sustaining consistent high moral character with others, are aware of when they slip up, and are quick to make corrections reflecting their core values. When we are dealing with leaders with integrity, we are much more likely to trust them because we know what they stand for and are confident that they will act in ways that are consistent with those values and beliefs. Leading with integrity is successful because it creates a sense of safety, a sense of optimism, and a sense of constancy and direction.

Most of us have experienced the destructiveness that can result from working for or with someone lacking integrity. Most often, we start out believing what they say and trusting that they have our best interests in mind. When their actions reveal deception or frank self-interest, we experience betrayal. The trust that is built over time is shattered and extremely difficult to re-establish.

From a communication perspective, one can think about integrity in terms of how often a leader acts in accordance with their word (i.e., how seriously they take their verbal commitments). According to Erhard, Jensen, and Zaffron:

> Honoring your word as we define it means you either keep your word (do what you said you would do and by the time you said you would do it), or as soon as you know that you will not, you say that you will not to those who were counting on your word and clean up any mess caused by not keeping your word. Honoring your word is also the route to creating whole and complete social and working relationships. In addition, it provides an actionable pathway to earning the trust of others.

Whereas every leader struggles to cast themselves as visionary, heroic, and ethical, their practical actions may belie these self-beliefs.

In actuality, we become what we repeat, not what we imagine ourselves to be.

Practically speaking, caring about one's integrity goes one step beyond the conscious communication we have been advo-

In actuality, we become what we repeat, not what we imagine ourselves to be.

cating in this book, to include a psychological and even philosophical exploration of one's character and commitments. Great leaders are self-aware and communicate a sense of wholeness and high moral character in everything that they do. Moreover, when they deviate from their values and commitments, they are quick to acknowledge their missteps, take responsibility, and engage in corrective action.

VULNERABILITY

One of the reasons leadership today is so challenging is because all organizations and institutions—from churches to banks to universities to hospitals to local governments—exist in highly ambiguous, turbulent, dynamic environments. This high level of turbulence makes a mockery of long-range strategic planning and puts pressure on leaders to constantly evaluate their goals and make sharp corrections when needed. Successful leaders today must be able to quickly admit when they have made a mistake and change direction. For individuals who are "invested" in the idea that they know everything and don't make mistakes, this can be a career-limiting challenge.

Great leaders speak comfortably about their lack of information, errors in judgment, and limitations. Strategically, this stance provides great competitive advantage and prevents organizations from "doubling down" on failing strategies simply because of some executive's ego or pride. Culturally, the willingness to be vulnerable in communication—to admit one's errors in judgment—legitimizes a climate where emotion, experimentation, and calculated risk-taking are authorized and even encouraged. Vulnerable leaders create a clearing for true dialogue and the consideration of multiple possible actions. Vulnerable leaders create psychological safety by modeling it with their own behavior.

Leading with vulnerability is a little like leading with a sense of good humor. Insecure, ego-driven leaders take themselves too seriously and would not be caught dead admitting weakness or errors in judgment. These leaders create humorless, fear-based cultures where defensive communication blocks learning and experimentation, and joylessness sinks employee engagement and morale. Secure, conscious, vulnerable leaders have a sense of humor about themselves and their expertise and are quick to admit where they struggle and where they have screwed up. These leaders shape balanced cultures where honest dialogue promotes learning by expanding and where people are both willing to try new things and are happy to come to work.

HUMILITY

In the end, the beautiful thing about leadership is that it cannot be forced to happen. One can believe they are a leader and then be surprised to learn that no one is following them. Humility is key to effective leadership because in the end it is not really about you. Instead, leadership is all about creating an environment where people feel as if they can work together to accomplish great things that they could not have done alone.

Humility is key to effective leadership because great leaders leverage what is all around them to channel energy toward amazing outcomes. Humble, conscious leadership is not about "muscling" things to happen. Like the moment one becomes aware of the fact that the secret to a handstand is alignment, not strength, leadership is about alignment, leverage, and connection.

Experienced, successful leaders eat last and speak last. They use silence and inaction to create opportunities for followers to step forward and share their gifts.

Many authors have tried to identify the most important qualities, competencies, abilities, traits, and habits of successful leaders. Some have even acknowledged that humility is important. We propose that humility is more important than any of the competencies or qualities that have been studied. Humility appears when one begins to empty their cup. Humility is the acknowledgment that "I could be wrong or my perception may be incorrect." Humility is the act of respecting that others may know more than I do. Humility is the key to engagement because any pursuit of engagement while believing I already have the answers threatens to be a farce. Humility cannot be commanded from employees or leaders. Humility can be practiced. Leaders need to be seen as humble. Employees, by virtue of the example they see, come to their own conclusion that the leaders genuinely display humility. Leaders have opportunities to practice humility every day. Learning to become more conscious and curious about communication demands humility.

Once a critical number of leaders and teams become conscious of how communication works, this consciousness goes viral. In conscious organizations, leadership is personal and leaders are committed to sustaining one another's elevated consciousness. Feedback is valued, not threatening. Employees look forward to their leaders showing up in their work area. Annual performance reviews become more like pit stops on a five-hundred-lap race than an end-of-race assessment. More clarity about goals emerges as a greater result of extended conversations than from delegations and proclamations.

Many books about leadership identify the importance of "walking the talk," which refers to a leaders ability to behave in ways that are consistent with their espoused vision and values. We would like to add that as communicators, leaders must also "talk the walk," by which we mean they must be purposeful in creating aspirational narratives that help employees make sense of how actions—both the leader's and their own—connect to the organizational mission and vision.

New employees are hired because of their expertise, competence, and humility and are therefore more predisposed to continuous learning. Employees become able to let their respective leaders know they are interested in career development without fear that they will be retaliated against for their disloyalty—everybody is in it for each other, not just themselves. The focus of meetings becomes outcomes, not performing or reading off scripts. Leaders who understand communication are better able to engage their staff and are more present. Such leaders personally feel more engaged in their work, in the lives of their employees, and in the life of the organization. Everyone is a meaningful member of a team. The sum total of a conscious organization is improved clarity, understanding, and performance.

We have felt challenged to find ways to help influence and support changes in communication practices that increase positive outcomes. We acknowledge these positive outcomes are not academic theories. Positive outcomes are about real experiences of customers, patients, and families. The approach we recommend improves outcomes for people and the organization. When applied, it can contribute to improved quality control, fewer medical errors, fewer accidents, and fewer deaths across many industries. Leadership is about developing and working toward a preferred version of the future, an aspiration that attracts others to pursue. Leadership is never about coercion.

Great leadership is about creative collaboration, not compliance and control—fostering a common understanding of the nature of the work and a shared sense of responsibility and collaboration. Leaders need to nurture a climate that is more about seeing what is actually happening and being willing to talk about it in the pursuit of an honest present, a healthy communication climate—a safe environment with more people concerned about doing the right thing than about being judged or worried about the politics of impression management. In this healthy, conscious organization, people stop protecting their positions or imagined credibility and start focusing on authentically supporting their teams and delivering quality.

PART FIVE

Stories of Practice, Lessons Learned

CHAPTER TWELVE

Bringing the Principles of Conscious Communication to Life

We have thus far described the core principles of conscious communication and offered multiple strategies to apply these principles in daily life. This chapter contains true stories of how we have applied conscious communication to specific clients who either sought us out or were required to seek our assistance by their leaders.

In the introduction to this book, we commented that we would provide you with a comprehensive way of thinking about your own development as a leader focused on three major processes:

- Conducting an honest self-assessment focused on your level of self-awareness

- Clarifying the choices/decisions you make regarding your communication and your relationships

- Designing and applying a continuous improvement process for your leadership and for those you lead

Sometimes when we explain these three processes of conscious communication to clients, we introduce a mnemonic as a memory aid. Specifically, we advocate for "APT" communication, which requires:

1. Awareness

How do clients currently communicate their self-awareness, other-awareness, how and what they give their attention to during conversations.

2. Pause and Presence

Does the client pause or immediately respond/react in conversations? How quickly does the client respond/react to others' comments? To what extent does the client engage in self-talk while participating in discourse? Is there a purpose or intent to what is said beyond taking turns expressing one's self? Does the client communicate in the present tense?

3. Testing and Continuous Learning

Clients learn they need to own the coaching sessions and that they are responsible for their learning and for sustaining their progress. They must, therefore, learn how to experiment with their behavior and measure it against conscious communication principles to continuously improve during and after the coaching sessions. To do this, they learn how to observe other's reactions as naturally occurring feedback, how to solicit feedback, and then how to use their feedback to incrementally improve their real-time conscious communication effectiveness.

For each of the coaching interventions that follow, we describe the background situation for context and then show how conscious communication and the APT methodology was applied. We have the highest regard for our client's confidentiality and have, therefore, made changes in these stories to protect our clients' privacy. The outline for each story is as follows:

- Client

- Situation

- Duration of Consult

- Our Work
  - Awareness
  - Pause and Presence
  - Testing and Continuous Learning

- Outcome

This chapter contains stories about ten clients:

CLIENT 1

Japanese female physician (Dr. L.) who received her medical training in the US, working in a New England hospital for three years.

Situation

Dr. L. had developed a reputation for being abrupt, short, aggressive, and even hostile to nurses, orderlies, PAs, consulting physicians, and members of her own team. Dr. L.'s supervisor had received over a dozen written complaints, which were shared with Dr. L.

Dr. L. dismissed all complaints, describing nearly everyone who complained about her as incompetent. Her supervisor worked with human resources, and they coauthored a ninety-day performance improvement plan. If there was insufficient progress after ninety days, she was to be terminated.

Dr. L. disregarded the plan because all she cared about was her patients. Her patients loved her. After ninety days, there was not enough progress, so her supervisor and HR gave her another ninety days. After 180 days her supervisor saw little improvement yet did not want to fire her because of how much appreciation she received from her patients.

Dr. L.'s performance problems were then escalated to the senior physician executive for the hospital whose first reaction was "I thought she was fired months ago." The senior physician executive invited me to a meeting of all the people who had been involved in trying to help Dr. L. improve her performance with her coworkers. While most of the people in the room wanted her fired immediately, several people in the room believed that if she could just change her communication behaviors, she could be an awesome physician. The senior physician executive said, "We have given her enough chances to improve. It is time to let her go." I asked, "If several people in the room believe her problems are a result of her poor communication, has anyone with expertise in this field worked with her as of yet?" The answer was no. I was invited to work with her for six weeks. Her supervisor facilitated the introduction.

Duration of Consult

Coaching intervention: Five ninety-minute meetings over five weeks

Our Work

Awareness: During our first meeting she described her primary concern to be her patients. She spoke disrespectfully of nearly everyone else who supported her patients, describing them as simply her "arms and legs" when she could not see them immediately. Anything that went wrong or that was suboptimum was their fault. She was heavily committed to telling me stories in which she was the victim.

One of our primary goals during a first encounter was to create an environment of psychological safety and trust. I allowed her to talk (nonstop) for about fifteen minutes. I then interrupted her to ask if she was aware of how she was treating me, if she felt she was treating me respectfully, and if she had any interest at all in learning if and how I might be able to be of assistance. She became quickly aware that she was using our time together to vent—to vent about past situations for which she was consistently the hero and everyone else was the villain.

Much of our first session was spent inviting her to become more aware of her words, her tense (past, present, future), where and what she gave her attention to, and what she was feeling. Eventually she was able to understand that I was trying to understand how she communicates with others based on how she was communicating with me. She shared her fears and vulnerabilities with me. She said that she believed the other people she worked with did not like her. She helped me understand that she was working with many misunderstandings about how perception and communication works, and she felt certain that she was right.

Pause and Presence: Using a variety of figure-ground exercises during our second meeting, Dr. L. came to realize that her first impressions might not be accurate. We did a "what else could that mean" exercise to begin to expand her awareness. We explored "what if" the people to whom she was being dismissive were actually trying to help her and her patient. She shared that at the beginning of our coaching sessions she believed she was the only person who cared about the patient. While this may appear preposterous, we have found there are no limits to the manufactured opinions and conclusions people can create in order to hold on to the belief that they are the heroes of their own stories.

- I shared the standard stimulus-response theories with her as a normal organic process. All living things are subject to stimulus-response patterns. Human beings, however, are the only living organisms with the capacity to pause before the response. We explored her reactivity to others as knee-jerk reactions and conclusions. As one example, if someone says, "Can you cover my shift on Friday night?" she could react by saying, "How dare you assert your Friday night is more important than mine, you jerk." Or she could be curious and respond, "I am not sure. I can check my calendar. Sounds like something came up. I hope you are OK." Rather than shoot back answers, the slightest pause gives us the oppor-tunity to thoughtfully direct our response toward learning more, being kind, and accomplishing something.

- Gradually, over a couple of meetings, we spent more and more time in the present tense—communicating with each other rather than taking turns tossing words back and forth. Another exercise that seemed useful for her was to invite her to tell me stories about growing up with her family on their rural farm and to identify how those experiences impacted the ways she communicates with people today. To support her learning about the power of the pause, I also asked her what she learned from her different experiences and what else she might have learned. One of the problems with stimulus-response behavior is that it both promotes simplistic, single cause-effect thinking and closes our minds to multi-factor thinking.

- The more I worked with her, the more curious she became about how she could improve her ability to communicate without creating the collateral damage that seemed to follow her. At one point she appeared ready to learn about consciously communicating with someone in order to accomplish a goal, which we have also called communicating more strategically—to accomplish something, not just to express herself. She learned that when she speaks with people, she can either choose to bark at them or engage them. She can inspire people rather than threaten people. Best of all, she can learn to observe people's responses to determine her effectiveness, this is real-time feedback in action. After each coaching session she was given homework that required her to begin experimenting with new ways of communicating to practice at home, with people she trusted, and eventually with all the people she worked with.

Testing and Continuous Learning

During meeting number four, she dramatically improved communication with me and began telling stories about her improved communication with others. As she related these stories, they were filled with specific behavioral observations of how others were responding to her both verbally and nonverbally. She was progressively discovering that she could improve her communication success with others. Her care for the patients continued to show up in our conversations as if she was either the only one who cared, or she had to believe that she cared the most. Sometimes her need to express her care for patients seemed to be out of context with our conversations, though I felt it must be in the context of her thinking. I focused on what she thought caring meant to her, what makes it important to restate this point, and what else she cares about. While giving me a list of what she cared about, she became very emotional.

She described caring for patients, their families, their needs, their outcomes. Then I asked her to describe what she did not care about. She began naming people she works with—orderlies, nurses, technicians, housekeepers—and then she began crying, repeating the words, "I cannot believe I have not cared about them—they have families, they have children, they have been patients at some point in their lives, they, too, are doing the best that they can, just like me."

During our last meeting, meeting number five, she described the differences between how she used to communicate and how she communicates now. She and I practiced her new behaviors and she provided several stories about how, in addition to communicating patient information to nurses (for example), she also communicated her respect and appreciation for their work.

Outcome

This consult took place in 2016. Dr. L. continues to be a highly regarded physician who now has excellent communication skills. Everyone, including the senior physician executive, appreciates her work.

CLIENT 2

G.S. was employed as the chief executive for a public utilities company based near Boston, Massachusetts, for about a year and a half.

Situation

At a board meeting that G.S. was unable to attend, the board agreed that they would not renew his two-year contract when it expired. Board members had been receiving complaints about him for several months—he was condescending, aggressive, insulting, disrespectful, and intimidating. His staff had reported that they did not trust him. Without an intervention, G.S. would have received a poor written evaluation, and his contract would not have been renewed.

One of the board members contacted me and asked if I could try to help him—he would continue to be in charge for six more months, and any improvement would likely not change the planned outcome though it might reduce some of the hostilities in the company. The board member specifically asked me not to tell G.S. that his contract was not being renewed. Since most of the complaints about G.S. appeared to be connected to his interactions with colleagues and direct reports, I offered to meet with him. I asked the board member to contact G.S. and invite him to meet with me because my communication expertise might be useful to him.

Duration of Consult

Coaching intervention: Two meetings over three weeks

Our Work

Awareness: During our first meeting, after describing how I assist individuals in improving their communication effectiveness, I asked G.S. to describe how he communicated with others. My intent was to engage him and observe how he communicated with me. For more than half an hour, I found myself impressed with the way he said he spoke to his employees, peers, and board members—and the way he was speaking with me. I tried and failed to see him as condescending or offensive in any way. In fact, he appeared to possess integrity, vulnerability, and humility—which ultimately enabled him to learn how to make improvements very quickly.

To continue and refine my observations, I increased my attention to his nonverbal communication and noticed a pattern. After taking a few minutes to validate my observations, I made the following observation to G.S.:

"It appears to me that you have been constantly working to hold eye contact with me and that you may do this with others in both lighthearted conversations and intense ones."

His response:

"Yes, you are absolutely right. When growing up, my parents taught me that the only way to show respect to others was to hold eye contact during a conversation."

I offered that it was important for him to know what that kind of intense eye contact felt like to most people. As an experiment, I held eye contact with him for ten minutes. He then volunteered that it felt intimidating, forceful, almost threatening.

During the remainder of our first session, I explained how eye contact works during human communication. I also explained that it has different meanings depending upon a person's culture—in many cultures, displaying eye contact conveys disrespect. One of his errors in the context of conscious communication was that he believed that if he had a working definition of the value of eye contact, then everyone else probably thought the same way.

Pause and Presence: His homework assignment was to increase his awareness of his efforts to make and hold eye contact. In our next session, he continued his learning about how the meaning of ideas is conveyed in communication—it is decided by the receiver. He learned that he needed to pause several times during conversations to observe what he was doing, what he wanted to accomplish, how he wanted the other person to feel after the conversation—such as respected, challenged but not threatened, optimistic, and appreciated.

Testing and Continuous Learning: We actually practiced this learning several times during our second meeting. He quickly learned how to modulate both the use of eye contact and its intensity. He saw, understood, and demonstrated that nonverbal communication complements verbal communication. If they are ever in conflict with one another, such as when the speaker feels appreciative toward the receiver, yet the speaker's eye contact seems intense and critical, the nonverbal cues usually win. His homework assignment was to continue to practice brief reflective pauses (the duration of a breath) during conversations to inventory his communication goals and both his verbal and nonverbal strategies. He called me a couple of weeks later with examples of his progress. I determined no additional meetings were necessary.

Outcome

Complaints deceased. At the end of his two-year contract, he received an outstanding performance review, and his contract was extended for an additional two years.

CLIENT 3

Mr. C. had risen through the ranks of a major defense contractor to become program manager of one of the largest military aircrafts ever made. He came to us because he was experiencing a great deal of stress and struggling with time management.

Situation

Mr. C. retained our services because he wanted to learn time management skills to better cope with the stresses of running a major military manufacturing program.

Duration of Consult

Coaching intervention: Three months of coaching, with sessions every two weeks

Our Work

Awareness: In order to better understand the challenges Mr. C. was facing, we requested to attend his regular staff meetings and operational briefings, as well as to conduct some more general observation of communication in his office suite. At one critical meeting, he had asked each of his ten direct reports to summarize recent accomplishments and challenges to an assembled audience of about fifty managers and directors. This meeting was held at a time when the program was experiencing heavy pressure from the Department of Defense regarding the excessive weight of the aircraft.

Most of the operational updates were routine and went unremarked, but one individual described a series of decisions that clearly upset Mr. C. Rather than let him finish his report, he interrupted angrily and scolded him in front of the group. "How in the world could you have made that decision? Didn't you even bother to think it through? How could you have such poor judgment?"

After these remarks there was an eerie silence, as if you could hear everyone in the room thinking: "Don't let that happen to me."

Pause and Presence: Following this fateful meeting, we showed up at the appointed time for our coaching session with Mr. C. Our meeting was delayed in starting because there was a line out the door of people waiting to speak with him. When we did begin our meeting with him, we were frequently interrupted by managers who wanted to "just check" with him about various decisions they were about to make. He used all of this activity as an illustration to us of what he had defined as his time-management problem. But we saw it differently.

We inquired about the angry exchange in the meeting; he sought to minimize it, saying that he blew off some steam because he, like everyone else, was under pressure, but that there was no lasting impact. We suggested otherwise and asked him to reconstruct the incident from his employee's perspective. "What was the employee seeking to accomplish in his report, and how did he hear your response?" Once he gave it more thought, he came to realize the chilling effect it might have had on that person and everyone else in the room. We suggested that his "time-management" problem might actually be the result of his employees being frightened to make an independent decision because they did not want to be embarrassed in public.

Testing and Continuous Learning: Over a three-month period, we attended several meetings and provided our impressions about how his communication was perceived by his employees. He came to understand that while in his head he was "easygoing," when under stress he could be quite cutting and mean. The result of that kind of communication had a chilling effect on his entire team. Once he became aware of this pattern—what he came to call his stress communication style—he was able to recognize it early and refrain from treating employees that manner.

Outcome

Mr. C. gained awareness and control over his communicative choices, which caused his "time-management" problem to lessen considerably as employees became confident in their ability to make independent decisions.

CLIENT 4

J.S., employed as an information technology support technician in a hard-driving information technology firm who, after two years, established himself as a high-tier outstanding technician well known for his abrasive, insulting, and sometimes hostile behavior toward the executives that he was sent to help.

Situation

The person managing J.S. tolerated his offensive behavior because of his exceptional technical skills. J.S., therefore, learned that his behavior was acceptable. The reputation J.S developed (as a technician and as a short-tempered, offensive individual) continued to grow, until a very specific management meeting took place with his manager, director, and vice president. It seemed that J.S. had great potential to lead a team and to train them to also become superior technicians, if only for his attitude. J.S. had insulted and offended so many people that his job was now at risk. If he was unable to change the way he behaved, he would be terminated.

One of the options was to begin progressive discipline—a process that could take three months. Three more months of his behavior, even if making incremental improvements, was unacceptable. The VP requested a consult, and, given that all of the challenges appeared to be directly related to his communication skills, we tentatively accepted him as a client. Our first meeting was with J.S. and his manager.

Duration of Consult

Coaching intervention: Four sixty-minute meetings over six weeks

Our Work

Awareness: During the first meeting, the manager, J.S. and I introduced ourselves. When I described my role, I explained that I was not sure if I could be of assistance and that the more I understood how J.S. communicates with his clients the better I could let them both know if and how I might be able to help. I asked J.S. to share some stories about his work. While inviting him to tell stories, I was more interested in how he engaged me in the conversation.

His first story was about an executive whose computer had slowed to a snail's pace. J.S. went to his office, politely introduced himself, and said he was there to fix the computer. The executive said "OK, I just need to finish making some entries." After a short period of time, J.S. started swearing at the executive, raising his voice, and throwing insults at him. After all, J.S. also had a job to do, which did not include waiting for the executive to do his job on a faulty machine. J.S. shouted for the executive to get out of the office.

During this story telling, J.S. told the story as if reliving it. He appeared very emotional, angry that he could not do his job, angry that the executive reported him for having a bad attitude, and angry that he had to meet with me for "be nice to people" coaching. During his story telling, J.S. was abrupt, intolerant of simple requests for background information, and judgmental, certain in his beliefs that it was the executives who needed to respect him. A popular phrase that could be appropriate is that it seemed J.S. had the proverbial chip on his shoulder.

By the time we got to the second story, I told J.S. that I needed to talk to him about how he was communicating with me. He seemed defensive and hostile. I learned that he thought he was about to be fired and we were just going through the motions to collect as much evidence on him as possible.

In the present moment, I chose an opportunity to make a point—that he was behaving toward me based upon his conversations with himself, his beliefs about what was going to happen. He was operating from beliefs that he never checked out. He believed that his opinion about what was going on in a conversation was the only reasonable opinion for anyone to have. He believed the executives he was trying to help were condescending and lazy thus wasting their time and his. By the end of our first meeting, he realized that all of his behavior was based upon his own untested assumptions about other people's motivations. His homework was to take some written notes after some of his service calls, notes that would enable both of us to study those conversations and try to track the escalation. J.S. was technically brilliant. Asking him to analyze conversation patterns piqued his interest.

During our second meeting, I was able to interrupt him to point out his nonverbals, his use of "but" and blaming, his avoidance of responsibility, his push-back language. He became aware of his reactive pattern of communication—more reactive to his internal conclusions than the actual behavior of the people he spoke with. By the end of the second meeting, he became curious and was committed to studying his own behavior.

Pause and Presence: In order to meaningfully study (pay attention to) his own behavior, I believed it was time to introduce or mirror his reactivity. During our third meeting we reviewed the behavioral stimulus-response patterns of all living things. He seemed to appreciate that it was normal for people to react to situations. He found it a little difficult to accept that only human beings have the capacity to pause between the stimulus and the response and choose a path that is planful rather than reactive.

He did not know that he did not know he had choices—he could choose his responses. We practiced this behavior in the present tense by role-playing a few of his stories and giving him opportunities to change the endings of those stories. We explored his need to pay attention differently, real time, when supporting people, and we worked out a question that seemed to work during our role-plays: "I am certain I can figure out what is wrong with the computer. I need to figure out what my client needs—what does this person need right now?" While this seems like a long question, he can verbalize it in his mind in less than 1.5 seconds.

Testing and Continuous Learning: During our last meeting, his first story affirmed our approach was working. In his own words:

"I had a ticket for an executive with a computer that had a very dim screen. I showed up and introduced myself and was shocked that after the executive came to the door to invite me in, he sat back down at his defective computer. I felt angry. I was there to fix the computer, and why was he sitting at it. So I paused and asked myself, 'What does he need right now?' Rather than express my anger with the executive, it occurred to me to ask him if now was a good time for the service call or if he wanted me to come back later. [Note: throughout this process, J.S. was learning about himself.]

"The executive told me that he needed my help right away, though he continued trying to do his work on it. I then asked him if solving his computer problem might help him get his work done faster. The executive paused and said, 'That is a great idea. Let me show you my problem.'"

Fixing the computer took J.S. less than three minutes. The executive was very appreciative. J.S. added, "When I left my client's office, I paused outside of his room and imagined myself punching my fist into the cement wall. How could he not know that I was there with the skills to fix his computer?" J.S. told me that it was in that moment that he realized everybody pays attention differently, and the most important skill in his work was being able to pause when others' behavior does not make sense to him and to strategically figure out how to respond to situations that get his clients what they need—including a fixed computer.

J.S. described a few more of his cases with similar outcomes. After his stories, we practiced more situations in the present—I played the role of angry, frustrated, irritated, impatient clients. He demonstrated his capacity to pause before reacting. As part of our role-play, we practiced multiple strategies to help him become aware of the wide range of choices available in every situation.

Outcome

Three weeks after our last meeting, the manager called to express his joy at the customer service skills J.S. had learned. J.S. and I never used the phrase "customer service." We paid attention to helping him become more conscious of the communication process—of his and his client's needs, of his ability to pause and strategically lead the conversation to a positive outcome. Six months later J.S. was promoted.

CLIENT 5

The absence of humility and vulnerability can be profound. When a highly specialized physician has integrity without vulnerability and humility, there will likely be many communication problems. Dr. L.M. had a reputation for superior work with patients and dramatically offensive and hostile treatment of staff, especially residents. Both his position and his career were at risk if he could not make improvements in the way he treated others. Two residents informed the department chair that they resigned because of Dr. L.M.

Situation

Dr. K., the chair of an advanced area of specialization in a New England hospital, called me to describe a desperate situation. Two of his four residents had quit this past year. In a hospital, a resident is a person who has completed medical school and often some advanced specialized education. To be a practicing physician, he/she must now complete three or four years of residency at a teaching hospital, depending upon the area of specialization. Much work by the organization and the applicant is involved. Having circumstances that lead to even one resident quitting is not good for the people involved or the residency program. Losing two residents compromises the ability to attract the best candidates for the following year's program.

Dr. K. was absolutely certain he knew the reasons his two residents resigned; the problem was Dr. L.M. This physician had been employed for four years, was excellent in his specialization, served as one of the faculty for the residency program, and had a reputation for high-quality work with patients. His lack of vulnerability and humility left him highly resistant to any feedback, coaching, or even friendly suggestions that might have been able to help him. Dr. K. contacted me to explain that a new group of residents was starting in his department in two weeks, and Dr. L.M. either had to be helped before they arrived, or he would be terminated. Dr. K. could not afford to lose any more residents. Dr. K. was particularly frustrated that his attempts at counseling and coaching were unsuccessful. With respect to conscious communication, Dr. K. was unaware that somehow his behavior had sanctioned or reinforced Dr. L.M.'s behaviors. Nevertheless, he was asking me to work with Dr. L.M., not himself. Here is how Dr. K. described the two major problems with Dr. L.M.:

- Dr. L.M. has profoundly bad breath. All of the areas throughout the hospital where he works keep a spray bottle of odor-removing sanitizing spray on hand in case Dr. L.M. uses one of their house phones. Allegedly, if he uses a phone for more than a minute, the mouthpiece smells from his bad breath. Dr. L.M. was unaware that people were spraying down phones after he used them. He was also unaware of people's expressions when he spoke with them as they tried to suppress their reactions to his intensely bad breath. After Dr. K.'s description of this concern, I offered to address it with Dr. L. M. only if it showed up during our meeting. I explained that I would not accept responsibility for coaching someone about past behavior that may no longer be part of his current situation. If he showed up with bad breath for our meeting, I agreed to resolve the problem. Otherwise, this concern was Dr. K.'s to address when it occurred, real time.

- Secondly, Dr. L.M. has some communication problems: seen as condescending, aggressive, intimidating, overpowering, insulting. When asked for concrete examples, Dr. K. shared several. Dr. L.M. interrupts his residents when they give report after almost every sentence. He criticizes them publicly; he reprimands them for not knowing things (they are residents because there are many things they do not know). They are there to learn, not to be humiliated; he frightens nurses to the point that several go out of their way to avoid interacting with him, including hiding from him when he shows up on their floor. And yes, this does create a risk for his patients.

Dr. K. believed this physician was unusually resistant to the kind of coaching he had provided to other staff for many years, perhaps because of his culture.

Given Dr. L.M.'s responsibilities, we would be able to meet for only one hour in each of the two weeks remaining before the new group of residents arrived for their first day of orientation.

I agreed to work with Dr. L.M. on two conditions: Dr. K. had to give him a direct order to meet with me for the two hours (one each week), and Dr. K. had to inform Dr. L.M. that his employment was at risk if he failed to make substantial improvements as a result of this coaching. Dr. K. agreed.

Duration of Consult

Coaching intervention: One hour a week for two weeks

Our Work

Awareness: We met in a private conference room. Dr. L.M. was a couple of minutes late. He walked in, sat down, and informed me that he had been told to meet with me, though he was unsure about the reasons. When I attempted to introduce myself, he cut me off so that he could complete his rehearsed introduction of himself. Then he said, "I am done now. You can speak."

I briefly described the work that I do and explained I wanted to get to know him a little bit because I was not sure what was going on. I told him that I was not sure if I could be helpful. (I also was not sure if he wanted any help, a prerequisite to any potential future behavior change.) For about ten minutes he explained that all his problems were other people's fault. He asserted he was expert at providing patient care. He described that he was a victim of incompetent residents who blamed him because they lacked the intelligence to continue in the program. He also displayed considerable nervousness and/or anxiety as he was unclear what was supposed to happen during our meeting. When he summarized his stories, he said that there might be some way he could improve his relationship and teaching skills and that he was open to improving himself. This last line sounded more like he was reading it from a teleprompter than as something coming from his heart.

Given our work on conscious communication, the most useful information I learned from Dr. L.M. during his ten-minute lecture to me was the way he treated me. He showed no awareness of the impact he had on other people. Some descriptors that could apply here include condescension, arrogance, absolutely certain his perceptions were correct, and others were wrong, constantly looking at the wall clock as if his orders were to sit with me for an hour as opposed to try to learn something from me, disinterested in me—who I am, what my interests were. After about ten minutes, I interrupted him. Note that I generally prefer to invest more time in getting to know clients; however, our total available time together was limited to 120 minutes, and I felt the need to use every single second as constructively as possible.

I told him that in the interest of time I wanted to interrupt him so that I could check in with him as to how well we were doing in this meeting. He said OK. I told him that I was curious as to what he thought my first impressions might be of him. He responded by telling me that there is no such thing as first impressions. He is who he is, and my opinion was of little or no value. I persuaded him that the science I have studied consistently has shown that human beings often do have first impressions and that these first impressions occur upon first contact and then over the first three to four minutes of conversation.

He acknowledged that he did experience first impressions, and he agreed to answer my questions.

My first question: "Dr. L.M., what do you think my first impression is of you?"

He replied: "I believe you see me as an expert in my field, an accomplished physician, and someone who is interested in improving my teaching skills."

My second question was: "Dr. L.M., on what data do you base your conclusions that this is the most likely way that I see you?" He replied: "You would see me as an expert in my field, an accomplished physician and interested in improving my teaching skills because I told you these things about myself."

I told him that it was time for me to share something with him that he might not be aware of, that was potentially scary for him to hear: "It appears that you believe my first impression of you is that you are an expert in your field, an accomplished physician, and interested in learning more about teaching wholly based upon your observation of your own behavior, again, based only upon observations of your own behavior. As such, if you believe you are interrupting me to teach me something and I feel defensive, humiliated, insulted, etc., the only logical conclusion is that your behavior was instructive (as you see it), and my reactions are hallucinations.

"Dr. L.M., I fear you have somehow created a delusional world in which you are the hero of all your stories. If you continue to believe others have opinions about you in strict compliance with the impressions you think you are giving them, then your success both as a physician and in all your relationships will be significantly compromised." I shared that he appeared unaware of how communication actually works and unaware of how to improve.

I asked him if he wanted to know what my first impression actually was. He said yes. I told him that I experienced the following behavior:

- Arrived late, no apology

- Came to meeting wearing dirty, wrinkled, disorganized clothes with a shirt collar that looked like a clown collar with the tips curled up (no collar stays)

- Began talking, taking over the conversation with no apparent opportunity for me to say anything

- Gave me permission to speak

- Spoke with air of superiority, potentially intimidating

- Revealed zero vulnerability and humility

Halfway through our first meeting, I gave him a choice: "If you are satisfied basing your beliefs as to how effective you are with other people by observing your own behavior, I believe you are being delusional and want to continue being delusional, and we have no further need to meet. If, on the other hand, you would like to learn how to observe other people to find out how effective you are as a caregiver and teacher, I can teach you how to observe other people so that you can know how they perceive you and use that information to get better at everything you do." I left him alone for a couple of minutes to make his decision. When I returned, he said he wanted to live in the real world rather than his delusional one.

Pause and Presence: For the remainder of our first meeting, we focused on his awareness of his behavior—he realized that when he talked to people, he was seemingly throwing words at them. He realized he was not looking for reactions or feedback that would show understanding or lack thereof; his only goal was to get his words out and move on. He realized he was judging his success with others based upon how much he talked and monopolized air time, not on whether or not anyone grasped what he said.

He discovered that he needed to pause periodically to check in with the people to whom he was speaking in order to find out if they were on the same page. He learned that speaking to express himself could often come across as an arrogant lecture and that speaking to accomplish something for someone else is a much more useful goal. As a teacher, speaking to show off what he knows is completely different than speaking in such a way as to help his residents learn. He began learning about goal-oriented conscious communication. His homework was designed to increase his attention to others' needs and interests.

Testing and Continuous Learning: Dr. L.M came to our second meeting in what appeared to be a new suit with a dry-cleaned and starched shirt. He said that he wanted to learn more. After debriefing his homework, we engaged in rapid-fire role-playing in areas that we both agreed were high priorities. With respect to interruptions, I told him a story about my cat and asked him to interrupt within the first minute of the story. About a minute into my story, he interrupted, saying, "Well, I had a cat named Fluffy, and he was a lot of fun, he …" He interrupted my story in order to tell one of his own. I called a time-out, and we replayed the role-play trading places—he played me and I played him. After I interrupted him to say, "Well, I had a cat named Jacob …" I asked him how it felt. He replied, "You stole my story!"

We revisited communicating with purpose, and he agreed his interruption style was to steal others' stories and take over. We practiced a variety of ways to interrupt that show respect and advance the other person's story. With each passing minute, he began accepting that his expertise in his own field was extraordinary and, because of his communication weaknesses, probably came across to others as not respecting them for their expertise in their fields. He began checking in with me for my perceptions of his behavior. He discovered he had options he had never imagined. He became increasingly more curious about conscious communication and learned how to see other people's reactions to him as feedback for his own development.

Outcome

After two hours, Dr. L.M. learned to dramatically change his behavior with me and left with a plan to incrementally improve his communication skills with others. His chairman was able to immediately see the improvements. When Dr. K. eventually brought the "bad breath" concern to Dr. L.M.'s attention, he was appreciative and receptive to the feedback. It has been about five years since this consult. According to the chair, Dr. L.M. continues to be an excellent provider and is an outstanding faculty member for new residents.

CLIENT 6

Ms. H.B. had been a manager in her department for over seven years. After attempting to find a qualified director for her area for nearly a year, the senior vice president of the area approached Ms. H.B. and asked her to consider stepping up. She agreed as long as the SVP could arrange for some coaching—becoming a director, she believed, would be challenging.

Situation

The SVP believed Ms. H.B.'s greatest challenge would be communication—with her employees, with her new peer group, with senior members of the organization, and with members of the community. We were contacted to provide that support. Ms. H.B. had an excellent reputation. The goal of the coaching was to support her transition to director.

Duration of Consult

Traditional coaching: Eight months. Initially meeting every other week and progressing to monthly meetings after three months for the duration of the engagement.

Our Work

Awareness: When we first met in Ms. H.B.'s office, she was about five minutes late. Her first words were "I'm sorry I am late. I was stuck in a meeting that I could not get out of." I assured her I was not worried about being a few minutes late; I knew she was very busy. I was, however, curious that her first words were of apology, not a greeting like "Hello" or a positive expression of appreciation like "Thank you for coming" or "I am glad to see you." I decided that bringing my concerns to her attention during our first meeting would not be productive—she was already nervous and somewhat anxious in her new role, and she wanted to look strong during our first meeting. I invited her to catch me up with her story, a beautiful success story. I spent much of our meeting answering her questions about my work as a coach and reassuring her that I believed she would be successful.

Part of my initial assessment was that she apologized a lot to everyone; that she did feel trapped in a meeting she could not get out of, as opposed to having the confidence and self-assurance to decide to stay for the remainder of the meeting because it was a business priority and then tell me that she was a little late because she decided to stay late at a previous meeting; and she used the word "but" frequently.

She shared that she did not know what she did not know. For the first few meetings I paid attention to the things she wanted to give her attention to. I gave her books, web sites, and applications for her phone to improve planning and answered her questions about how to engage her employees in making the best possible contribution to the organization. Based upon what she shared and how she shared it, I felt the need to make psychological safety a high priority for our long-term coaching relationship.

After those first few meetings, I began bringing things to her attention that were a complete surprise to her (she did not know what she did not know), such as:

- When you "but" your peers, they "but" back. However, when you "but" subordinates, they start shutting down, and when you "but" superiors they often take offense and do not tell you. Worse, most people "but" each other with no awareness of it, due to their habitual conversational behavior.

- No one can keep you at a meeting unless they are kidnapping you—you are always free to choose where to spend your time, and you are responsible for those decisions.

- When you establish an open-door policy, be certain that is what you want. When your employees come to you and you say, "I am too busy, come back later," you are acting contrary to your policy, and they may not come back.

The APT conscious communication process of awareness, pause, and testing needed to be repeated several times for each of the ineffective leadership habitual behaviors and beliefs that she was totally unaware of. For purposes of this case review in this chapter, I will focus on my efforts to help her to become aware of and permanently change her "but" behavior. I recommended that we begin exploring what she was unaware of so that once she became aware of it she would then have the ability to change it.

Our first "but" meeting began as did the previous ones. She had agreed to work on this behavior, so I engaged her in describing some of the meetings she attended. After approximately fifteen minutes, I asked her how many times she thought she had used the word "but." Her answer was "three or four." I had counted seventeen times. Please note, there is nothing wrong with this usage—as long as she is with peers and friends. In the presence of power differentials, the word can become a trigger for decreased psychological safety and increased tension and even censorship. The larger concern is that she was unaware of when she used this word.

To increase her awareness of her use of this word, I asked her, during our meeting, to begin writing a checkmark on a sheet of paper every time she or I used the word "but." A few minutes went by before she became self-aware when she was using the word during our conversation. Her homework was to track all "buts" by everyone in attendance at all meetings she attended over the next couple of weeks. She reported that she was amazed at the number of times the word was used, and she said that she was particularly disappointed at the number of leaders in the organization who used this word. She reported that she was disappointed because she was able to see the escalation of butting during the meeting. She also was able to observe decreased listening.

Pause and Presence: We should never underestimate the difficulty of showing someone a behavior they do not believe they do. Our goal was for her to substitute the habit of saying "but" with a new habit: pausing. To do this we practiced in her office. When she learned to pause rather than speak the "but" word, she asked me what I wanted her to do during the pause. We explored many possibilities, such as "Do I really understand what this person is saying?" or "What do I want to accomplish as a result of this conversation?"

Becoming aware was most important. Pausing is only possible when one is aware of their behavior. The actual self-talk may vary depending upon the circumstances and the people with whom she is engaged. The pause enabled her to speak intentionally, without the need to say "but."

Note that another version of managing a person's use of the word "but" is to teach them to substitute the word "and." This, too, requires awareness to be effective. If the person is unaware of saying the word "but," they are equally unaware of when to use the word "and."

Testing and Continuous Learning: Ms. H.B. enlisted the aid of people she trusted to continue to increase her awareness of her "but" habit. Given the nature of her work, she was involved in many meetings and had multiple opportunities ever day to practice new behaviors and discern feedback from others' reactions.

Outcome

During periodic update meetings with her SVP, Ms. H.B. proved to be an excellent leader.

CLIENT 7

Senior Vice President J.B. needed assistance with two of her vice presidents, C.M. and S.F. Both vice presidents had been hired at the same time and had been working for eight months. Both had to work well together. Both complained to Senior Vice President J.B. that the other was not cooperating enough to make all the needed changes in their divisions. The client was J.B. The assignment was C.M. and S.F.

Situation

Multibillion-dollar organizations have goals and employ people at different levels of scope to both maintain their success and increase their value in the market. Two vital positions were created and filled in order to advance an organization's strategic goals. Two new divisions were created involving a total of approximately 125 employees. C.M. and S.F. were responsible for these divisions. As leaders, they needed to work out budgets, staffing (24-7), roles, deliverables, and ultimately the number and quality of services to customers. They needed "go live" dates for each incremental increase in service level. Their progress had been stalled. It appeared that each blamed the other for their lack of progress. The senior vice president did not want to start this business initiative all over. She needed a coaching intervention to enable her vice presidents to work together, best-case scenario, or determine which person would have to be replaced.

Duration of Consult

As a high-priority coaching intervention, C.M., S.F., and I met once a week for five weeks.

Our Work

Awareness: At the opening of our first meeting, I summarized the SVP's charge: "Enable the vice presidents to work together or she would decide which person would have to be replaced." Throughout this meeting, C.M. spoke in a measured tone, calmly describing their joint responsibilities for getting the resources, space, and budgets needed to plan and implement the goals they were assigned by their SVP. S.F. spoke in an accusatory tone, interrupting C.M. often and punctuating his comments with a variety of inappropriate and vulgar slang words. Each seemed super aware of the other's behavior and unaware of their own. The more calmly C.M. spoke, the more enraged S.F. became. In order to try to elevate their awareness of their own behavior, I asked them to identify any area for which they needed to make progress. They both agreed that one of the immediate needs was supplies—they had a common storage area for their resources. Staff from both their areas accessed the same storage area often taking more than what was immediately needed for fear that they might run out. I offered to give them about fifteen minutes without any interruptions to make some kind of progress so that I could try to learn how I might best be able to help. At the end of the fifteen minutes no progress was apparent. I asked each of them to describe what they had done to attempt to move their discussion toward improvement. Each only wanted to talk about the other's perceived resistance to any kind of compromise or negotiation. They reported they were at an impasse.

For my next meeting, I met with each separately. My goal was to try to enable them individually to be able to describe their own behavior during our meeting.

I modeled what I asked C.M. to do. I asked him some fact-finding questions about the supply room, including if employees were spoken with for their insights, what problems might be contributing to the overall impact of insufficient supplies, if they had a quality improvement process for mapping their supply chain, etc. Then I told him that I wanted to take a time-out for a moment, and I described my own behavior to him. I explained that for each question, I had choices as to how I asked it. I explained that we cannot improve our own behavior if we are unaware of it. We cannot exercise choices if we are unaware that we have choices. C.M. was then able to continue the conversation about the business problems and when I called a time out he was able to describe his behavior.

During my meeting with S.F., I repeated my approach. S.F. was not able to describe his behavior. He said the exercise was just a silly waste of time and that the real problem was that C.M. was incompetent. He refused to cooperate and told me that he was certain J.B. would fire C.M.

Pause and Presence: Our third round of meetings also took place one-on-one. At the outset of the meetings, I shared some relevant research on negotiation and conflict management. C.M. was accepting that he was responsible for exercising self-control during conversations with S.F. and periodically pausing (just for a breath or two) to choose his words strategically to try to advance their progress.

During my meeting with S.F., he asserted that the research I had brought was useless, and our meetings were a waste of his precious time. He said that he was responsible for getting real work done. I proposed to him that the larger problem was communication. I explained that resolving his communication challenges with C.M. was a prerequisite for solving the work issues. He began swearing at me and reiterated that I was wasting his time. This was an excellent opportunity to bring to his attention that I was now interested in his ability to communicate with me. He repeated that I was wasting his time and that his senior vice president was not smart enough to know what he needed. He said that he needed to be in charge of both of the areas and that he would just tell everyone what to do. His behavior was aggressive, demanding, insulting, and foul by any standards. He was unaware (and uncaring) that other people had different perceptions and that a little collaboration could go a long way. He asserted again that no collaboration was needed, only making everyone do things his way.

Based upon his behavior, I paraphrased what he had told me and then terminated the coaching relationship. I then arranged to meet with both people I was attempting to coach and the SVP to provide the reasons I ended the coaching relationship.

Outcome

Within the week, the four of us met. I described the work that I had done and invited C.M. and S.F. to agree, disagree, or amend. Both agreed with my description. Both agreed they were at an impasse. S.F. then criticized SVP J.B. for wasting his time. He added that all of this warm, fuzzy stuff was irrelevant and that he alone knew what was necessary. He used his colorful language filled with expletives. I apologized for not being able to accomplish SVP J.B.'s goals. J.B. thanked me for my attempt and asked me to leave the room and wait for her in the lobby. About ten minutes later she met separately with me to explain that although the coaching appeared to be unsuccessful, in truth, it provided her with all the information she needed to make a decision. S.F. was removed from his position the following week.

CLIENT 8

Dr. S.B. had an outstanding reputation for patient care and research in a central Massachusetts hospital. He also, allegedly, had some anger management issues which were ignored because of his excellent work.

Situation

One summer Friday, Dr. S.B. reportedly picked up his computer monitor and threw it into the middle of the room, frightening several people. He also did some shouting. By the end of the day he was sent home for a full week and told to make dramatic improvements when he returned. He was given the names of several people who might be able to help him with the needed changes. On Sunday morning, the day before he was to return to work, he called me and asked if we could get together that Sunday afternoon because, he explained, if he showed up at work on Monday morning without being able to have more control over his anger issues, he believed he would be terminated by the end of the day. We agreed to meet in a town green—a beautiful part of town with much attention given to the lawns and many gardens.

Duration of Consult

Coaching intervention: One two-hour meeting followed by two one-hour meetings over a two-week period

Our Work

Awareness: We sat on one of the benches by a garden and gazebo. After a brief introduction, I invited him to share what was going on. During his explanation he became agitated and angry. He described that he was a victim. He explained that he had become frustrated because "those people" in the information technology support department were of no help, and he could not take care of his patients because of all the problems with the electronic medical records. I asked him if he was aware that he was becoming angry while we were sitting in a beautiful place. He defensively argued that was not his fault—just thinking about all the problems delivering quality care was nearly overwhelming. I invited him to take a breath and to try to calmly describe one specific problem.

Dr. S.B. told me this memorable story: "My computer makes me so mad. I had a waiting room full of patients at noon a week ago Friday, and it would not work right. I needed it to update my patients' records real time. They have to get their prescriptions; I have to enter my notes. That machine was so slow it just pissed me off."

I asked him if I could repeat the story back to him the way that I had heard him explain it to me and he agreed: "So you, a brilliant physician, with a track record of securing grants and providing outstanding patient care and research in your specialty, believe your inanimate computer laid awake all night thinking about ways it could deliberate provoke you and then you showed up to work and it kept failing at the worst possible time, on purpose, just to make you mad. You did say your computer made you mad." He laughed.

I proposed, can we agree that the computer is inanimate, and if so, where did the anger come from?

His language and awareness became much more refined. He described being frustrated, being worried about his patients, feeling like a failure not being able to provide for them the way he wanted to. Before my eyes, he let go of his anger and described his anxiety over his ability to do his work. The anger, he proposed, came from himself, not the computer. He seemed to understand that his anger came as a result of what he was paying attention to, not from an inanimate object on his desk.

I asked him to help me better understand where his anger comes from, now that we know it is not the computer on his desk. He explained, "It is very simple. When two people hold different positions, the truth is in the middle and I have to always fight to get what is right. I hate having to lose ground in an argument. My patients lose if I settle for middle ground." I asked him how long he had believed this, and he replied, "My entire adult life."

I shared with him that I felt sad at hearing his description of where his anger comes from. He seemed concerned at my honest expression of feeling sad and he asked me where the sadness came from. Responding to his question, I explained that it appears he, a great doctor, a husband, a father, a teacher had spent most of his life believing something that simply was not true and has, as a result of that belief, lost out on countless opportunities for collaborations, joy, and successes that he can never get back. I offered to give him a demonstration that would show him what I meant, and he agreed.

I pointed to a plant in the nearby garden and asked him to describe to me what he saw. He said, "I see a beautiful flower, burnt orange, sitting amongst the green leaves." I then said, "I see bug-eaten rust-colored petals of a once-beautiful flower that would be dead by morning." Dr. S.B. was one of the truly brilliant people that I ever had the opportunity to work with. In response to my different observation he said:

"Wait a minute, your description was different from mine, your description is not wrong, mine is not wrong, there is no middle ground between our positions. Everyone's perceptions of what they see is just different. The more people looking at a situation, the more different perceptions there may be. The truth that I had said was in the middle between positions cannot be true. Rather, the truth is something that includes all the different positions. Different does not immediately translate to opposing."

He became aware that at least some of his understandings about anger, positions, and communication were wrong and he expressed a sincere interest in unlearning other beliefs that could be getting in his way. He willfully committed to emptying his cup and learning about the importance of vulnerability and humility in human communication.

Pause and Presence: Rather than engage in more storytelling, we mutually created opportunities for us to disagree while strolling through the garden, in the present. His capacity to process what I was sharing with him was extraordinary. I then introduced the "pause" to him and offered to give him the opportunity to respond to challenging situations in ways superior to how dogs, cats, squirrels, and other animals react to their environment. He quickly accepted that only human beings had the capacity to pause between stimuli that may appear threatening and how we choose to respond.

I asked him to give me a real-life example of an interaction that had "set him off." He described a conversation with someone from the tech-support department at the hospital where he worked. He had called the "help desk" because his log-in password was not working. The support person asked him several questions to verify his identity (computer security is paramount in health care), and he became irate. He had called the help desk earlier in the day, and he acknowledged, in his story to me, that he assumed the person he just called should have remembered him from an earlier call. It never occurred to him that different people answer the same phone number in a call center.

He realized while telling this story that he made several incorrect assumptions while the help desk representative was just trying to do her job. He said that now he wanted to apologize, but he would never know which person to apologize to. Before talking about how to apologize to people, a future concern, I asked him to try to stay present with me, right now, and retell the story attempting to discern when he felt his anger rising in the story and visualizing when a pause could have been helpful.

He retold the story a couple of more times, each time a little differently and then he got visibly excited. He explained to me that he was angry with the help desk, not the service representative. He speculated that if he paused after connecting with someone whose job it was to be helpful to him, the most respectful thing he could do was to learn the person's name and tell him/her that he appreciated their expertise. During this conversation he theorized that his pattern of being angry was always with things, departments, nonspecific "those people," not individuals. He believed if he became aware of the person's name, he would not become angry. He understood awareness, the value of the pause, and the need to practice the communication principles that I had introduced to him.

Before leaving that first meeting, he asked me how many months of meetings it might take for him to be able to change. I told him that his question was another example of something he needed to unlearn. If he believes it will take eight months for him to learn, it will take eight months. If he believes he has already changed, then he has already changed. (I said this to him in this unique situation; this is not true of all clients.)

He agreed to put into motion all that we had discussed and then meet for a couple more times so that I could help him calibrate how to use his new conscious communication skills. I asked him to bring me examples of his application of these principles at our next meeting.

Testing and Continuous Learning: One of the examples he shared with me was about his work with the help desk. He had immediately put this into practice on his first day back at work. He asked the person who answered the phone for his name. Dr. S.B. wrote down the name and called the person by name several times during the call. Dr. S.M. expressed his frustration at his own skills, that he was embarrassed by problems he could not figure out. They talked about the immediate problem at hand, resolved it, and then explored what might happen the next time. The Help Desk representative suggested Dr. S.B. might benefit from some consistency so they made arrangements for Dr. S. B. to call the help desk and ask for a specific service representative over the next couple of weeks; not all Help Desk calling centers have the flexibility to do this. By working with one consistent person, they both realized that at least some of Dr. S.B.'s problems came from some problems in his computer.

Outcome

Dr. S.B. was retained. He is a nationally recognized award-winning expert in his field. His organization and patients are grateful for his hard work and excellent communication skills.

CLIENT 9

Dr. E.D. was chair of the emergency department in a large city for approximately one year.

Situation

The hospital had spent a year looking for someone with his credentials; his honeymoon period was over. He was reported to be belligerent, aggressive, obnoxious, condescending, unapproachable, insensitive to other's needs, and constantly offensive to finance, quality, nursing, and several other departments who needed to work closely with the emergency department to provide the best care for the hospital's patients. He always believed his opinion was correct, that he knew more about his technology needs that the information technology department; knew more about his budget than the finance department; and knew more about nursing than the nursing division. His arrogance and bloated self-confidence seemed to have no limits.

In a private meeting with the senior medical officer of this organization, I was given detailed descriptions of Dr. E.D.'s behavior as observed by his peers, senior leaders, and members of his own department. I was told that despite his expertise, if he did not change his behaviors within thirty to sixty days, he would be asked to leave—which could undo many of the contributions Dr. E.D. had made for the hospital. More important, and highly sensitive and confidential, the senior medical officer explained that he himself had failed at coaching Dr. E.D. It was also important that any coaching with this chair be strictly confidential. If some people found out that he was being coached, such could compromise his authority and/or expertise as well as the organization's ability to encourage him to seek employment elsewhere. I asked the senior medical officer to set up the meetings so that Dr. E.D. and I could meet discreetly.

Duration of Consult

Coaching intervention: Four one-hour meetings over four weeks

Our Work

Awareness: During our first meeting, my first goal was to double-check that Dr. E.D. and I were working with the same instructions. Dr. E.D. did confirm he had been told the same that I had been told. Once confirmed, Dr. E.D. assured me that the senior medical officer's take on what was going on was completely wrong. In fact, he went on, everyone's opinion about Dr. E.D.'s work was wrong. Dr. E.D. seemed incredibly confident that only his perceptions were correct, about everything.

One of the strategies that I sometimes use to help others become more aware of how their perceptions and other people's perceptions can be different, without one being wrong and the other being correct. I showed Dr. E.D. some figure-ground images to show him that while even looking at an image on a sheet of paper, there can be two legitimate images that appear to two different people. He dismissed the exercise, pointing out that the image that he saw first was the dominant image and any secondary image was secondary. When people, therefore, saw the secondary image first, their perceptual skills were inferior to Dr. E.D.'s. Given his confidence, however misplaced, that his perceptions were always superior to everyone else's, I spent the remainder of the first meeting engaging him in present tense role-playing. My goal was to attempt to show him there were other legitimate points of view.

We tried two scenarios. I told him that I was going to ask him if there was any place I could get some water. I reiterated that I was not thirsty, that I was setting up a role-play in which I wanted to see if he could respond to me by saying, "It sounds like you would like some water, perhaps right now. Is that correct?" He agreed. I then said, "Dr. E.D., I wonder if there is any place around here where I might be able to get some water." He then picked up his phone and asked someone to bring me a water bottle. He did not paraphrase. He did not do a perception check. He acted on his belief that I wanted water right now. He did not notice that I was paying attention to how he interacted.

As a second attempt, I explained I was going to invite him out to lunch, as part of a role-play. I specifically said that after I invite him out for lunch, I wanted him to say something like "It sounds like you think it would be good if we could spend some time together more informally. Is that right?" Dr. E.D. agreed. I then said, "I would love to have lunch with you some time." His response was to go to his computer calendar and say, "How about Thursday at 1:00 p.m." His responses showed me that he acted on what he heard, and he had no reservations whatsoever that he could be wrong. In his mind, he was always right. He did not know what he did not know, and it seemed he did not want to know. My need, for his benefit, was to increase his awareness of things that were not in his awareness.

During our second meeting I invited him to share what he considered his best and worst relationships. He shared only challenging relationships. Unfortunately, his list included his wife and children. He told me they were tired of him always needing to be right. Despite this painful experience within his own family, he still could not see that other people legitimately process the world differently than he did. During this second meeting, I asked if I could video record some of our role-plays and then delete the recordings when the meeting was over. He agreed. With the camera rolling, I told him that I wanted him to repeat back to me exactly what I said to him beginning with this instruction. He said, "OK." I said, "Then do it." He said, "Do what?" I said, "Repeat this phrase. Quote, 'repeat back to me exactly what I say to you beginning with this instruction,' closed quote." He said, "OK."

I then played the video back to him and showed him that the word "OK" was not, in fact, a repeat back. I easily persuaded him that "repeat back" was an established procedure to confirm understanding during handoff training, and it appeared to be something that he was incapable of doing. He said, "Why repeat back? I heard it the first time and know what was said." I pointed out that he only thinks he knows what was said, and he could only be certain if he repeated it back and I said, "Yes, that is correct."

After a few similar exercises, I asked this question, which proved to be on-target for his needs. "Would you rather advance the conversation because you are certain you heard correctly or double-check what you heard by paraphrasing or summarizing what you were told and potentially finding out your first impression was incomplete or wrong?" His honest answer was "I like being right, so I really do not want to run the risk of being wrong by paraphrasing or double-checking what I heard someone say."

I asked him to repeat his answer back to me several times so that I could be sure he was fully aware of the implications of his answer. The second or third time he repeated it back to me, he said "Oh my God! Is this what I have been doing to people?" I explained yes, he had been misunderstanding people's intentions by deciding what their words meant and then holding them accountable for his interpretation of their words. He accepted that the first words he speaks are essentially a rough draft of the ideas in his mind. I offered whether it was disrespectful of him to not extend the same belief to others. Is it not fair to hear what someone says, and double-check their intent, their meaning, their conclusions, their direction before expressing agreement or disagreement or even before requesting others' input? He was now aware of a critical dynamic in communication—perception equals perception, not certainty. To leverage his new awareness, he needed to learn how to pause and think about how to learn other's intentions as opposed to freezing their words and not allowing them to share more about their ideas. We continued to practice with the video recordings.

Pause and Presence: Pausing did not come easy for Dr. E.D. His medical school training was to be decisive and he feared being indecisive or even curious about other's thinking might make him look weak as a leader. I offered that his logic appeared to be a very useful way of defending indefensible behavior—refusing to hear people out, refusing to help others express themselves more fully so that he could benefit from the expertise they brought to the table.

Testing and Continuous Learning: The behavior changes I had invited Dr. E.D. to make were substantial. They had the potential to impact his family, his work, and his life from this point forward. During our meetings he also needed some additional learning about feedback, humility, leadership, engagement, and more. We continued practicing his learning during our last two meetings, until he reached a point of competence and confidence. Nevertheless, he had already begun modifying his behavior. Once he was aware that he was causing harm, he could not continue to do such. As we wrapped up our coaching relationship, he began asking about books and journals that would help him continue to develop his communication abilities.

Outcome

Two weeks after our last session, I received a confidential call from the senior medical officer. He said, "This past week I received phone calls from three executives in the organization who work closely with Dr. E.D. They wanted to know if I knew if he was on some kind of medication. I asked them what they meant. Each of them told me that seemingly overnight, Dr. E.D. no longer cuts people off, no longer tells people they are wrong. He even summarizes what people say and asks if he heard them right. He seems patient, considerate, collaborative. It is so different from how he normally behaves, we feel worried about him." Dr. E.D. worked for four more successful years as chair and then, with his family, relocated to another organization to advance his career.

CLIENT 10

Mr. E. was hired as a manager because of his expertise in his field. Senior leadership was committed to long-term investments in the organization's leadership continuity, and this individual was selected because of his high potential to move from manager to director to vice president within two to three years.

Situation

Over the course of Mr. E.'s first year and a half of employment, his leaders began to worry that they had selected the wrong person both for the position and their hopeful career trajectory. Mr. E. had tendencies to work in the weeds, to micromanage, to speak to subordinates as if they were his personal employees as opposed to hardworking men and women with different roles, responsibilities, and talents. He did not seem to be able to show respect for the members of his team. One of his leaders confided to me that he actually appeared to be dismissive or even disrespectful to support staff. Mr. E.'s leaders reported they were confused when he seemed so capable when presenting to senior leadership. They wondered how such a respectful person could treat some people with disrespect.

Mr. E.'s leaders shared they were thinking about plateauing him and looking elsewhere for their future director and vice president over this area of the organization. Before locking in this decision and initiating a new recruitment process, his leaders asked if we would be able to provide an assessment of Mr. E.'s communication/relationship skills and his potential to make substantial improvements in this area. We agreed on the condition that our coaching be required, a condition of employment.

Duration of Consult

Coaching intervention: one ninety-minute meeting and four one-hour meetings over six weeks

Our Work

Awareness: In preparing for this coaching consult, Mr. E.'s leaders made it clear that there were some challenges around the way Mr. E. treated people. Rather than come to any conclusions based upon other people's observations which may or may not be accurate, I created an opportunity to observe Mr. E.'s behaviors when encountering a wide range of people (organizational level, gender, attire, accent, role, etc.). When Mr. E. arrived at our meeting room, I greeted him, introduced myself, and let him know that I was thirsty and wanted to go to the office building café in the basement. I invited Mr. E. to join me and offered to get him a cup of coffee. He said that he would be happy to go with me and that he would take care of his own coffee. Our meeting room was on the twelfth floor. We encountered a lot of people on our way to the basement café. Mr. E. greeted almost no one—except for the vice president who joined us to travel down a few floors. The VP was greeted with "Good morning, how is your day going?" The VP politely replied.

When we reached the café, it was crowded. I selected a bottle of water for myself and greeted several people, most of whom I did not know. Mr. E. quietly got in line to make his coffee and spoke to no one. The line to the cashier was about five people deep. When I reached the cashier, I commented, "Is it always this busy around here this time of day?" She laughed and said that I had just missed their quiet time by about five minutes. While she was speaking, I looked around her work area and saw some family pictures, apparently with her and her young children. I then added, "That's a great picture of you and your kids. You look very proud of them." She beamed with appreciation and told me their names.

This entire conversation took place while I was paying for my bottle of water and she was getting me my change. When I was cashed out, I took a few steps away (staying in earshot) and waited for Mr. E. who spoke not a word to the cashier. We encountered many people on the elevator going back to our meeting room. I initiated friendly conversations with several. Mr. E. said nothing to anyone.

When we returned to the meeting room, Mr. E. asked if we could get started by going over some of his stories that might help me understand the kind of coaching he believed would be helpful. I told him that would not be necessary.

Pause and Presence: I explained that I found it most useful to work in the present, or at least as present a situation as was possible. I told him that I felt he had already done an excellent job of showing me some of his leadership weaknesses. I stressed, from the very beginning, that he appeared to have some communication habits or automatic pilots that would limit his success as a leader, and I felt my job was to help him become aware of these challenges so that he could have the choice to stay the way he was or to make improvements. We reviewed several of his behaviors—how he treated people, what impressions they could reasonably have of him. One of his first lessons was that he cannot not communicate. He mistakenly believed that if he did not speak, he was not communicating. He had no idea that his nonverbal communication was shouting out, "I think you are not important." As he began to replay people's reactions on the elevator to me and their reactions to him, he quickly became aware that he had a substantial knowledge gap about communication.

I asked him to try to replay both my and his interactions with the cashier. His memory was excellent. He retold the description of our conversations identically to my own memory. He told me that I was polite, that I engaged the cashier in small talk, that she smiled when I was speaking with her, that it appeared we knew each other (it was the first time I had met her), and then he said that he said nothing to her. We had already established that communication involves much more than just the spoken word. I asked what conclusions the cashier might have been inclined to come to about me and then about him. He resisted this learning; it can be very difficult to empty one's cup of what they think they know already. He said that she would not have come to any conclusions about him because he said nothing.

He then revealed a personal belief that could guarantee he would never be promoted in his organization. He said,

"Sean, you do not understand. The cashier is nothing to me. She cannot do anything for me; she is just a cashier. There is no reason for me to be nice to her. She's just handling cash transactions; that's her job. After all, why would I waste my time being nice to her?"

We spent the remainder of our first meeting processing his statements to me and my recommendations.

We were fully present, no more stories about other people, just him and me in the room. He was telling me that he lived with conclusions that I found offensive. He judged people he did not know. He looked down on people. He valued people in proportion to what they could do for him. He believed that he could hide his beliefs about people by not speaking. Functionally, he was describing a belief system to me to justify his behavior. The more he talked, the more he revealed he was very shy, easily intimidated, afraid of people judging him, afraid he might say the wrong thing.

In an effort to avoid getting distracted by his memories, his lifetime of self-talk justifying his behavior, and his burning desire to rationalize why he is the way he is, I revisited the pause and the present tense several times. I invited him to experience what it feels like to give respect to others without expectations. I invited him to be nice to everyone he meets and see what that felt like.

Essentially, I invited him to challenge all of his hierarchal, judgmental, and condescending behavior toward others by pausing while he is contemplating being quiet and asking himself "What can I say or do to show respect—to everyone?" For most people, we recommend they pause before speaking. For Mr. E., he needed to pause before he made the decision to be silent for even when silent, his attitudes leaked out through his behavior and most could see/sense it. Rather than talking about pausing, we began spending time on the elevator, not going to the café, but rather simply going up and down, for several trips.

Sometimes he had only two flights to begin and end a positive conversation with another passenger, sometimes ten or fifteen flights. He experienced what it was like to engage people, versus ordering them around. He found out that most people were hardworking, caring, and talented. He learned that different people have different talents. He grew to want to learn more about others and to respect that each person has his/her own journey. If we have the opportunity to help someone else on their journey, it is the right thing to do.

Testing and Continuous Learning: The transformation was dramatic. He continued to practice pausing. He asked himself better questions during his pausing, such as "What does this person need? What could I say that could help this person feel recognized for their great work? What outcome do we need from this meeting?" He called me every six to eight weeks for what he called a "refresher."

Outcome

His leaders began receiving compliments about his relationships, rather than complaints. One year later Mr. E. skipped the director position and was promoted directly into a vice president position, where he was successful for many years.

****

In an effort to underscore the value this work has had for us, we have not written it to express ourselves and then be done. We are not sharing the skills in this book as a set of merit badges to be accumulated and displayed on a sash. Rather, we want to accomplish something, in you.

The subjects in this book have been prepared the way a chef prepares a meal. The chapters are intended to be digestible, with appetizers flowing into the main course and then dessert. You'll read about sometimes humorous, sometimes entertaining, and sometimes surprising discovery stories on how good people learned some things they needed to unlearn in order to use heightened awareness, pausing, and self-correction to grow to a more powerful and humble level of leadership. The skills we describe, if we are successful, will be internalized. For us, conscious communication is a way of life.

When we coach someone, we learn from them. When we teach in the classroom, our students are an endless source of excitement and enthusiasm. Every group of students enable us to learn more about our own patience, flexibility, and innovation. We have many opportunities in our lives to practice these skills.

I remember one such time when I was stuck at an airport—many flights were being cancelled. This was my first time spending the night at an airport. It felt like only half an hour had passed since my flight was canceled, and while figuring out where I needed to go, the concourse filled with four or five flights of people in a line that stretched out forever. That was the line I needed to be in.

My first thought was to call home and let my family know that I was going to be a bit late coming home and that when I did get home in the next day or two, I would probably be pretty tired. My next thought was to sit down and become aware of all my options. I had no reason to run into the line to cut ahead of other families. I had no need to rehearse desperate arguments that my needs were greater than other people's. So I paused and asked myself three questions: What can I learn from this experience? Who might be interesting to meet? What good can I do right now, right here?

I had recently updated my prescription lenses, so I scanned the space and enjoyed seeing. I could clearly see things that were very far away, things that only a couple of weeks ago would have been too fuzzy to appreciate. I saw some food options I would have missed. After a while I began to notice the frantic airline employees bracing for a lot of unexpected yet predictable work. They had done this before. Yes, they knew what to do, though working with angry passengers cannot be one of the most enjoyable parts of their jobs. I proceeded to the front of the line to scout it out. While walking there, I overheard dozens of angry, frustrated, unconscious communicators engaged in blaming people, working up their anger, and some even negotiating to advance their place in line. I also saw a few families having an impromptu picnic—they sent members of their family to get food so they could sit on the floor and have a spontaneous picnic right on the concourse. When the line moved, they just slid up to the new location, kind of like moving their picnic blanket.

When I reached the head of the line, I saw only three airline employees doing their absolute best to give each customer their undivided attention. I paused and asked myself, "What can I do that might make a difference for the employees and passengers?" I approached their desk from the side (not in line) and found a moment to say, "Excuse me." I told one of the employees that I was impressed at how calm they were and how careful they were at trying to meet every passenger's needs. I offered to get them all drinks (nonalcoholic, though we did joke about that). I can still vividly remember the expressions on their faces. I met several amazing people that night.

****

Striving to be more conscious communicators every day has brought us much joy and enabled us to be present at home and at work.

Knowing there is much we do not know, knowing how to pause, knowing to have purpose when we speak, knowing how to seek out self-correcting feedback, being willing to let go of faulty opinions or conclusions, all these things help us to *stop wasting words* so that we can make every day better for ourselves, the people we live/work with, and our clients.

About the Authors

ERIC M. EISENBERG, PHD

Eric M. Eisenberg is professor of communication and dean of the College of Arts and Sciences at the University of South Florida. As a global authority on effective leadership communication, Eisenberg has worked closely with executives and employees from organizations across a wide variety of industries, including Baystate Health, Big Y Markets, The World Bank, State Farm Insurance, Hughes Aircraft, McDonnell Douglas Corporation, Starwood Hotels and Resorts, Time Customer Service, Ned Davis Research, and Hillsborough County Government. Most recently, he has been offering workshops on strategic communication to members of the US Special Operations Command. He is an internationally recognized author, researcher, teacher, facilitator, consultant, and executive coach specializing in the strategic use of communication to promote positive organizational change.

Eisenberg's approach to interpersonal relationships was greatly informed by his two most favorite hobbies. As an amateur judo player he learned to tune in to the movements of others in planning his own actions and came to appreciate the philosophy "win by yielding." As an amateur musician, he learned how to cultivate "jamming" experiences that allow players to transcend individual achievements in the service of the success of the group.

Dr. Eisenberg received his doctorate in organizational communication from Michigan State University in 1982. After leaving MSU, he directed the master's program in applied communication at Temple University before moving to the University of Southern California. Over a ten-year period at USC, Dr. Eisenberg twice received the National Communication Association Award for the outstanding research publication in organizational communication, as well as the Burlington Foundation Award for excellence in teaching. He is also the recipient of the 2000 Ohio University Elizabeth Andersch Award for lifetime contributions to the field of communication. Dr. Eisenberg is the author of over seventy articles, chapters, and books on the subjects of organizational communication, health communication, and communication theory. His most recent academic work focuses on handoffs in health care and how improved communication can reduce the likelihood of medical error.

SEAN E. MAHAR, MA

Sean E. Mahar is a lifelong student of human communication. His master's degree is in speech communication from the University of Montana in Missoula with further studies in Gestalt psychology, healthcare management and delivery, and aikido. He worked for a large multi-hospital healthcare organization in western Massachusetts for nearly thirty years serving as director of organizational and professional development for ten of those years. He was also responsible for providing discrete coaching to nursing leaders, physicians, and executives to improve personal and organizational communication and performance.

For twenty years, Mahar also taught for American International College, Springfield, MA, as an adjunct professor for two of their graduate programs: MA in organizational development and MBA. His academic areas of expertise include negotiation and conflict in organizations, interpersonal communication, organization development, organizational behavior, and group dynamics. His hands-on expertise as a practitioner include enabling dramatic improvements in healthcare handoffs, behavioral interviewing, applying timely feedback to accelerate learning and performance improvement, executive coaching, and both leadership continuity and leadership development. He has shared his work in Massachusetts hospitals, via the Massachusetts Medical Society, and as a private consultant to business and healthcare leaders.

He has enjoyed opportunities (via Sean E. Mahar and Associates, LLC) to work with a variety of organizations including the American Association of School Personnel Administrators (AASPA), Overland Park, KS; Association for Business Communication (ABC), Irvine, CA; Association of Program Directors in Internal Medicine

(APDIM); Baystate Health, Springfield, MA; Human Resources IQ, Division of the International Quality and Productivity Center (IQPC); Loudoun County Public Schools, Ashburn, VA; Massachusetts Medical Society, Waltham, MA; Newport Classic, Ltd., Newport, RI; PLICO, Oklahoma City, OK; Shriners' Hospitals for Children, Springfield, MA; The New England Facial and Cosmetic Surgery Center, Danvers, MA; and Toyota Motor Engineering & Manufacturing, North America, Inc., Erlanger, KY.

Sean Mahar coauthored "The Patient Handoff: A Comprehensive Curricular Blueprint for Resident Education to Improve Continuity of Care" in *Academic Medicine*.

Sean, and his wife Deborah, have enjoyed raising their family in Western Massachusetts. Both their children participated in scouting and Sean is chair of the committee overseeing Boy Scout Troop 776. Sean loves music, occasionally DJing local events. He has enjoyed digital photography since it first made its appearance. He has been supporting regional community theater groups and his many friends with his portrait photography for over fifteen years.

Sean Mahar is a member of the International Communication Association (ICA) and the Gestalt International Study Center (GISC).

References

Vineet M. Arora, Ellen J. Bass, PhD, Leora I. Horwitz, MD, Sean E. Mahar, Ingrid Philibert, PhD, and Max V. Wohlauer, MD, "The Patient Handoff: A Comprehensive Curricular Blueprint for Resident Education to Improve Continuity of Care," *Academic Medicine* 87, no. 4 (April 2012): 411–18.

Marcus Buckingham and Curt Coffman, *First, Break All the Rules* (New York: Simon & Schuster, 1999).

Rob Cross and Andrew Parker, *The Hidden Power of Social Networks* (Cambridge, MA: Harvard Business School Press, 2004).

William R. Cupach, and Brian H. Spitzberg, eds., *The Dark Side of Interpersonal Communication* (Hillsdale, NJ: Lawrence Erlbaum Associates, 1994).

Frank E. X. Dance and Carl E. Larson, *Speech Communication: Concepts and Behavior* (New York: Holt, Rinehart, and Winston, Inc., 1972).

Joseph A. DeVito, *The Interpersonal Communication Book*, 8th ed. (Reading, MA: Longman, 1998).

Charles Duhigg, *The Power of Habit: Why We Do What We Do in Life and Business* (New York: Random House Trade Paperbacks, 2014).

Eric M. Eisenberg, A. Tretheway, M. LeGreco, and H. L. Goodall Jr., *Organizational Communication: Balancing Creativity and Constraint*, 8th ed. (New York: Bedford/St. Martin's, 2016).

Eric M. Eisenberg, PhD, and Sean E. Mahar, copresenters, "Communication APTitude for Leadership Success," Proceedings of Twenty-Year Conference on Organizational Communication: Traditions, Transitions, and Transformation,"

University of Texas, Austin, TX, 2016

Mark Gerzon, Leading through Conflict, How Successful Leaders Transform Differences into Opportunities (Boston: Harvard Business School Press, 2006).

Joyce L. Hocker and William W. Wilmot, *Interpersonal Conflict*, 3rd ed. (Dubuque, IA: William C. Brown Publishers, 1991).

Fredric M. Jablin and Linda L. Putnam, eds., *The New Handbook of Organizational Communication* (Thousand Oaks, CA: Sage Publications, Inc., 2001).

Muriel James and Dorothy Jongeward, *Born to Win: Transactional Analysis with Gestalt Experiments* (Reading, MA: Addison-Wesley Publishing Company, 1971).

Lynnete Elizabeth Johnson, *Only Love Can Do That* (self-pub., CreateSpace, 2015).

Robert Kegan and Lisa Lahey, *How the Way We Talk Can Change the Way We Work* (San Francisco: Jossey-Bass, 2002).

Mark L. Knapp and Gerald R. Miller, eds., *The Handbook of Interpersonal Communication*, 2nd ed. (Thousand Oaks, CA: Sage Publications, 1994).

Michael W. Kramer, *Managing Uncertainty in Organizational Communication* (Mahwah, NJ: Lawrence Erlbaum Associates, 2004).

Patrick Lencioni, *The Five Dysfunctions of a Team* (San Francisco: Jossey-Bass, 2002).

Sean E. Mahar, "The Centrality of Feedback in Teaching Business Communication and Improving Performance." Proceedings of the 2005 Association for Business Communication Annual Convention, 2005.

Frederick Perls, MD, PhD, Ralph F. Hefferline, PhD, and Paul Goodman, PhD, *Gestalt Therapy* (3rd printing 1980; New York: Bantam Books, 1951).

Thomas Sebeok, ed., *Animal Communication, Techniques of Study and Results of Research* (Bloomington: Indiana University Press, 1968).

Karl E. Weick and Karlene H. Roberts, "Collective mind in organizations: Heedful interrelating on flight decks." *Administrative Science Quarterly* (38), 357-381.